Invisible We See You

Invisible We See You

Tracing Celtic threads
through Christian community

Nancy Cocks

WILD GOOSE PUBLICATIONS
www.ionabooks.com

UK edition first published 2006 by
Wild Goose Publications,
4th Floor, Savoy House, 140 Sauchiehall St, Glasgow G2 3DH, UK.
Wild Goose Publications is the publishing division of the Iona Community.
Scottish Charity No. SCO03794. Limited Company Reg. No. SCO96243.
www.ionabooks.com

ISBN: 978-1-905010-29-5

Cover design © Wild Goose Publications

A catalogue record for this book is available from the British Library.

Printed by Bell & Bain, Thornliebank, Glasgow, Scotland

In gratitude

to the members of the Iona Community

who welcomed me so warmly

during my sojourn in Scotland

Acknowledgments

When I resigned my post as a professor and headed to the Isle of Iona to become Deputy Warden of the Island Centres, I called it "my mid-life adventure." I am indebted to many members of the Iona Community who took me on as friend and colleague during these adventurous years. The welcome and hospitality I received showed time and again how thoroughly Community members practise the values at the heart of their work on Iona which I recount in these pages. Three members played a key role in giving me the confidence to prepare this collection from resources I prepared for use in Iona Abbey. Jan Sutch Pickard, John Bell and Kathy Galloway are all inspiring preachers and remarkable poets whose leadership and friendship made my time on Iona sustaining. Each one encouraged me to find my voice in worship on Iona. Their support laid the foundation for this book.

I also want to offer my thanks to the islanders of Iona who shared time, wisdom and the occasional hearty laugh as they welcomed yet another stranger to island life. My life was also enriched and reshaped by members of the resident staff group with whom I lived and worked over three years. (Fifty-three of you by my count, plus the cat!) Their commitment and creativity provided many wonderful memories – and stories to tell. The hundreds of volunteers who came ashore in the same period, especially those who helped to make the MacLeod Centre an inviting place, brought insight and challenge that often inspired my worship designs. Deep peace of the Son of Peace be with you all.

Finally, my thanks to the editorial team at Novalis for their support in developing this book into something more than I first imagined. Kevin

Burns kept encouraging me to build the collection and frame it in ways that highlighted what I learned on Iona. Anne Louise Mahoney and her colleague Nancy Keyes did the copy editing to smooth out my turn of phrase, yet never intruded on the oral style of the text. To these three supportive readers I offer my deepest appreciation for confirming my conviction that good writing is always improved by good editing.

In the style of Iona Community undertakings, this book is the fruit of collaboration. The text has emerged from my fingers but the stories, songs and services have been shared. This is a book of the common life. May it bless as I have been blessed.

Nancy Cocks
Halifax, Nova Scotia
January 2006

Invisible we see You, Christ above us.
With earthly eyes we see above us, clouds or sunshine,
grey or bright.
But with the eye of faith, we know You reign…

Inapprehensible we know You, Christ beside us.
With earthly eyes we see men and women,
Exuberant or dull, tall or small.
But with the eye of faith, we know you dwell in each…

We are Your living temple,
by grace alone we are Your living body…

—from a prayer by George F. MacLeod
in *The Whole Shall Cry Glory*
(1985, Wild Goose Publications)

Contents

Introduction

Waking up to wonder

A hand tapped me on the shoulder.

I turned around to face a smiling stranger.

"You're the girl who preached in Iona Abbey on Sunday," he said, nodding eagerly.

For a moment, I was taken aback. In Canada, someone might have recognized me but no one would have called me a "girl"! Yet, here I was, waiting to board a ferry to the Scottish mainland, miles from anywhere I could call home. I did not expect to be recognized, but the stranger was right. The previous Sunday I had preached in Iona Abbey for the first time. I hadn't anticipated what my role there might mean.

I found my tongue. "Yes, I am," I smiled.

We chatted as we walked up the ramp to the ferry. This man, an English tourist in his early seventies, had come to the Abbey as part of a bus tour. Buses from the mainland scheduled their Sunday morning trips across the Isle of Mull in order to drop passengers at the Iona ferry in time to make worship in the Abbey.

"I'm not much of a churchgoer at home," he said. "But the Abbey is really something special."

Iona Abbey is truly something special. Steeped in centuries of history, it is surrounded by the stark beauty of the Isle of Iona. Lying off Scotland's west coast, Iona is a tiny island, three miles long and a mile and a half wide. Yet, for generations, it has been a place of Christian pilgrimage. These days it's also a popular bus-tour destination. My brief encounter in that ferry queue began the reflections that led to this book. That day, I was just a few weeks into a contract position with the Iona Community, one of its full-time staff working in and around Iona

Abbey. As a member of the resident staff, leading worship at the Abbey became a regular part of my activity. As one of the ordained ministers on the staff team, I often marvelled at the privilege of celebrating communion in that holy and historic space. My encounter with this eager stranger opened my eyes to the considerable responsibility that accompanied that privilege. Day by day and week by week, we invited constantly changing congregations of people from all over the world to engage the mystery of God's presence in worship. Neither staff member nor stranger could anticipate how any of us might be moved by our encounters in that special place.

"Invisible we see you, Christ above us." These words come from a prayer written by George MacLeod, founder of the Iona Community. MacLeod had a marvellous way of weaving strands from Scotland's Celtic heritage into his provocative and political prayers. It was humbling to think that some of my words would join his within the invisible tapestry of prayer woven by generations of worshippers at the Abbey. So often we enter worship aware of the broken threads and incomplete patterns in our own attempts to pull our lives together. Yet the longer I listened to guests and visitors on Iona reflecting on what happens in worship at the Abbey, the more I came to trust that God's Spirit would work with us there, no matter who we were or how we'd gotten there. Somehow we would be awakened to wonder. George MacLeod often referred to Iona as "a thin place" where "only a tissue paper" separates the material and spiritual worlds. The Spirit opens people's eyes in that holy place – not only to things we've never had the opportunity to see before, but also to things we have overlooked in our own lives. Above all, the Spirit awakens us to the invisible company of Christ.

Learning to see

One Saturday afternoon, I was walking from the Iona ferry to the MacLeod Centre where I worked, chatting with a newly arrived guest who had been to Iona many times. We walked slowly for she struggled with the inclines, resting on her cane from time to time. She also had trouble with her eyes, she told me.

"But every time I come here, I feel like I can see better. The light is different here. Maybe this time God will heal my eyes."

Her conviction was so deep! Yet, it wasn't an easy week. The weather was foul and the sea was rough. Not a great time for walking in the light she cherished. The conversation was good, though, and the week unfolded with its rhythm of daily worship, chores, program sessions, meals and quiet chats around the fire. We didn't have another chance to talk until the final evening, when her group reflected on what they were taking home from a week on Iona.

"New friends," said one. "Stones!" chuckled another. (The beaches of Iona are generous with their supply of sea-polished "gems.")

Then she spoke quietly, into a waiting pause. "I'm going home with a reason to go on living."

Her eyesight hadn't improved in those few days, but deep within, this woman knew what George MacLeod meant when he prayed, *"Invisible we see you, Christ beneath us."* She may well have met MacLeod on one of her earlier trips to Iona, for she had been coming to the island over many years. I encountered him only through his writing, however. There I found candour and a challenge in his words about the mission of the Church, and about how the Church often failed to attend to the world outside its doors. Like MacLeod, I am a Presbyterian minister, but one shaped by vast Canadian landscapes, not the subtleties of Scotland. Still, I was drawn to his prayers with their arresting images and powerful appeals that resonated not only with my love of language but also with my passion for faith that embraces God's hurting world. George MacLeod's vision for the Iona Community has inspired several generations of creative and committed ministries, not only on the islands of Iona and Mull but also in city cores and housing developments. In reading its stories, I sensed a community of companions in the Spirit, wrestling with the kinds of questions I met on the streets of my neighbourhood, too.

I originally came to Scotland to work as a volunteer with the Iona Community as part of its unique ministry of hospitality on Iona, to see what I might learn and share. I found myself drawn more deeply into the mystery of how God opens us up to fresh insight and new possibilities when we share "time out of time" with each other. I stayed longer than I had planned. I am not the first to have had my plans revamped while I was there. In that thin place, God will rearrange lives! Like the guest who found something she hadn't known she was looking for, I have come away from Iona with a new reason to go on in my ministry. Perhaps it is fair to say I have learned a new way of seeing, a new way of recognizing signs of God's renewing grace in the give and take of community life.

This book explores my reflections for worship and about worship at the Abbey as I take a second look at the three years I spent working and worshipping there. If you come along with me, we will be reading between the lines together, meeting some of the people who opened my eyes to God's Spirit at work in the nooks and crannies of this world. By spending virtual time on Iona in these pages, I hope we will also meet the invisible Christ, Word made flesh in both the ordinary and the extraordinary gifts of living in community.

A common surprise

In Canada, the Iona Community is known for its passionate commitment to justice-making and for its lively insights into worship and music. These gifts of the Community are shared around the world through its publications and by the work and witness of its members and staff. What is harder to share are the life-changing possibilities God creates when people join in a few days of common life at one of the Community's island centres. The centres invite people to discover who God is calling them to be, using a design that weaves friends and strangers together through worship, work, conversation and creative activities. Though a week on Iona will include holy space and prayerful times, we do not make spiritual retreats there in any classical sense of that term. Rather, guests and staff are challenged to look at the world afresh because of the person we've just met – at a meal table, climbing over ancient rock, or even cleaning a toilet! In this collection of resources, I hope to show readers some of the faces of Iona, faces of both friends and strangers. You are not likely to meet these folks in person, yet theirs are the faces beside you at your own bus stop, the very faces God wears to gain our attention.

> They caught me as I came into the MacLeod Centre after our morning staff meeting. One had bucket in hand, the other pulled off her rubber gloves, having just finished morning chores. "Could we see you today? For an hour? Even half an hour?"
>
> We agreed to meet just before lunch. I puzzled about this young couple over the morning. What made them so keen to talk?
>
> They were prompt. And eager. "We'd like to have a little service this week to reaffirm our wedding vows," he began.
>
> "Would you help us plan it?" she went on. "We don't know where to start."
>
> I had to catch my breath and think what to say. "Tell me about yourselves," I said. "Is there a special reason for a service this week?"
>
> The couple exchanged glances. She nodded at him. He began to tell their story. They'd been through a difficult patch. Pressure at work. Very young children demanding high energy at home. They'd drifted apart. An act of betrayal had led to separation.
>
> She took up the story. "We came here to decide whether or not we could go on together. And it's just amazing, what's happened. We want to stay together. We know now we can."
>
> He continued, "It's not just one thing that happened. But talking to other people, you know they can see a future, no matter what they've been through. And we can see a future together, too."
>
> That afternoon they planned the service, using prayer books and the language of love rekindling within them. It was my great honour to bless those vows in God's name. It was my delight to receive a picture from their family vacation a few months later.

This story gives you a little taste of life in and around Iona Abbey week by week. It points to the significance of setting aside our private worlds and preferred habits for a while, to take a risk on what God has in store for us. This couple experienced God's grace through the give and take between guests around the island centres. The Iona Community does not place any of its staff in the role of spiritual director or counsellor. Instead, the Community trusts that the direction of the Spirit will emerge when hearts open up to each other in the risky business of experiencing community. The common surprise during time spent together on Iona is how often God introduces us to the very person who has a word for us.

Both the Abbey and the work of the Iona Community inspired my writing on Iona. For readers who don't know too much about Iona, past or present, I want to sketch the layers of history and tradition that overlap in Iona Abbey before presenting the resources I developed there. I'll start with a glimpse of St. Columba and his work on Iona in order to set the Abbey itself and its later significance in perspective. Then I'll say a few words about the restoration of the Abbey in the twentieth century and how George MacLeod and the Iona Community became involved. Finally, I'll describe some of the current features of worship and common life at the Community's island centres, which provide the backdrop for the resources I've drawn together in this collection. Readers who are already familiar with the cast of characters at the Abbey and in the Community's centres may want to skip over these sections to the final part of this introduction. You'll learn more about how I drew these particular resources together and what I hope they can offer, beginning again with the section entitled *On Our Heads and Our Houses.*

To link the various fragments of history that follow, I've used phrases from services in the current *Iona Abbey Worship Book* as section titles. Many of these phrases come from Scripture, the spiritual source common to the many generations and traditions reflected in Iona's Christian history. However, this book doesn't intend to be a history of Iona Abbey or the Iona Community. For readers interested in more historical detail, there is a short bibliography of well-researched resources at the end of the book. I hope this glance through Iona Abbey's family album will help readers who are not as familiar with Iona keep the characters and generations straight.

The world belongs to God

The Irish monk St. Columba secured Iona's place in Christian history long before an abbey appeared on the island's landscape. In 563 CE, he set sail from Ireland with a few companions, eventually landing on Iona and choosing to settle there. Details of his journey have been obscured over the centuries, his reputation polished through the storytelling of faithful followers. Even his reasons for making the journey are disputed. Columba may have been banished from Ireland by his abbot for contributing to a conflict in which blood was shed. Then again, he may have set out on a pilgrimage as an act of commitment to go wherever God would take him, like many Celtic monks of that era did. Celtic pilgrims would truly have affirmed the words of Psalm 24, that the world belongs to God, as did their very lives. Columba had a powerful sense of doing God's bidding, whatever the truth of his motivation. He founded a community of monks on Iona that grew in significance and influence throughout the British Isles and beyond. Part of his influence was due to Columba's roots in an Irish noble family. The saint knew how to engage the leaders of his day! His faith also challenged him to keep moving into different regions of the mainland. Many holy sites in Scotland are linked to his mission travels, or to those of his students and successors on Iona.

There are just a few visible remnants of this early Christian settlement in the fields surrounding the Abbey, enough to make me pause in gratitude for the monks' tenacity to remain on the island in the face of a fierce climate and some equally fierce visitors. It takes a little imagination, however, to picture what Columba's community might have looked like in their daily life, praying at prescribed hours of each day (and night!), copying and illustrating manuscripts of Holy Scripture, growing crops and tending to the needs of pilgrims. It was not an easy existence. Yet this community continued its work and worship for at least 400 years after Columba's death in 597. However, Viking raids, which began around the coast of Britain in the eighth century, took a heavy toll on the monks over the years. One of the white sandy beaches on the north tip of the island is thought to be the site of a massacre of monks waiting unarmed to greet unexpected visitors, as their rule of hospitality required. The remainder of Columba's community finally withdrew from the island after another particularly gruesome attack in 986.

The Abbey as it now stands was not yet on the horizon, but through Columba's connections Iona had already become a centre and a symbol of Christian power. Its holy ground became the burial site for many generations of kings and chieftains from Britain and northern Europe. Their grave markers, which now rest in and around the Abbey, offer silent testimony to the skill of Iona stone carvers, as do the standing crosses nearby. The intricate knots and turns characteristic of Celtic design frame figures of influence, identities once well known now obscured by the effects of sea air on stone. The original burial ground, lying to the south of the Abbey, draws a regular tide of visitors looking for the definitive resting place of Macbeth, that famous Scottish king. However, it is also the resting place of the beloved of *this* generation. Iona's holy ground is tender and precious as much for those whose names and places are known to current islanders as it is for the prestigious ones of centuries past.

These stones will shout aloud

Construction of the Abbey was sponsored by the Lord of the Isles, Reginald MacLean, at the beginning of the thirteenth century. The ever-changing allegiances between chieftain and Church meant that the Benedictine order, not Columba's successors, was invited to establish its community on Iona. According to architectural historians, the Abbey was not built following the most common Benedictine plan. Likely the landscape of Iona's ancient "second beach" insisted on some of the Abbey's unusual features – cloisters to the north, the altar set much lower than the entrance. (The beaches of Iona were carved by ice age and wave action long before any human settlement took hold on the island. For the geologically inclined, I recommend a little reading about the ancient rocks, too!)

I love this building, perhaps because Iona Abbey has long refused to conform to anyone's convention. Its walls and floors show the dedication and decisions of so many generations – abbots, architects and artists of all sorts. It is the resting place for humble brothers and honoured elite; shelter for weary traveller and adventurous sparrow alike. There is faithfulness and patience in the very stones that have survived so many changes: a parable of God's faithfulness to humankind and holy patience with our commitment, which ebbs and flows like the tides of Iona. Even during the periods when the Abbey fell into disrepair, still pilgrims came. Stories from the nineteenth century recount small gatherings for worship within its crumbling walls, rafters long since rotted away. Iona has a holy pull, as contemporary visitors also attest.

> "Nancy, what are we going to do? A peregrine falcon is trapped in the Abbey."
> A worried staff member caught up with me as I waited on the jetty for the next boatload of guests one Saturday afternoon. By the time I reached the Abbey, someone had called a bird sanctuary for advice. Peregrine falcons are a protected species in Scotland. It might be coaxed down from the rafters with fresh meat, the expert suggested, once it got hungry. Until then, we should take care not to frighten this guest.
> I stood just inside the Abbey for a few minutes, watching. The huge bird swooped restlessly from rafter to rafter. I wondered who would frighten whom!
> To give the bird time and space to settle, we held worship in the Abbey refectory that night. In the morning, the bird was still in residence. We set up Sunday morning communion in the cloisters. The congregation gathered under the cloister roof and on the grass under open sky. "With earth, sea and sky, we sing

to you," we prayed. Thanks to the falcon, we took the measure of these words from the communion prayer in a new way.

Peregrine means pilgrim. This feathered pilgrim found its freedom later that day, an open window calling. Our windows on worship had been opened, too, as the Abbey invited us to stand before God once more in an unusual configuration.

Toward the end of the nineteenth century, the eighth Duke of Argyll began to plan the restoration of the Abbey church and set aside funds in trust for that purpose. Sadly to my mind, he died before he could see any of the reconstruction he sponsored. Traces from many generations are still apparent. A learned eye can distinguish the thirteenth century features from the fifteenth-century ones. Symbols carved in the stones tease out our guesses about their original meaning. The distinctive marble communion table and base to the baptismal font are two of the last fine pieces cut from Iona's own marble quarry early in the twentieth century. Around the major festivals of the Christian year these days, you are likely to see a splash of colour gracing the space with temporary insistence, courtesy of the current craft worker. The building's components are as eclectic as the people who gather there week by week. Somehow that's as it should be, I think. The Abbey is a living church with a long family history to tell. The Duke of Argyll envisaged that the Abbey should provide Christian worship "for all the churches," according to his trust, and re-established its presence without direct denominational affiliation. Today, worship designed and led by the Iona Community extends an ecumenical welcome, in recognition of that mandate. Groups from many different churches also plan services for the Abbey from time to time throughout the year.

George MacLeod's project at Iona Abbey began in 1938. He had a vision to restore the cloister buildings lying along the north side of the Abbey church. The cloisters symbolized for him the place of the common life where faith moved into action. The story of his vision and how it came together is inspiring, well worth reading beyond these pages. Just to set the scene for the Iona Community's presence on the island today, let me tell a bit of that story. During the 1930s, George

MacLeod was a parish minister in the Govan district of Glasgow. His parishioners languished amid unemployment and poverty as the Depression took hold in the shipyards of Govan. He sensed that the Church had less and less to say to people who were struggling to survive outside its doors. Wanting to make a difference, MacLeod began to create projects offering at least some temporary employment and a bit of tangible hope in Christ's name. In 1938, he brought his first crew to Iona to start the rebuilding project at the Abbey, combining those who knew the building trades with young men preparing to be ministers. The student ministers laboured alongside the tradesmen and shared a few months of common life, eating, praying and socializing together before and after work. Their conversations explored the tensions between the worlds of work and worship. The conversations that wrestled with issues around the meal table fed sermons and services that wrestled with issues around the communion table.

The Community as a network and organization began to grow out of the bonds of friendship formed during those first years of common labour. Those who worked together for a few months each year on Iona wanted to maintain contact when they returned to the mainland. Gradually, the buildings took shape in the face of many challenges – ongoing need for funds and material, World War II, suspicion within the Church, growing interest around the world. George MacLeod travelled a great deal to build support for this project. As construction continued over the decades, more people were drawn into the ongoing life of what had become the Iona Community. Work on the Abbey was completed in 1967, a testimony to the incredible commitment of all those men – and eventually women – who caught the vision that inspired George MacLeod. It is vital to realize that the energy for the work accomplished on Iona was sparked in Glasgow where different kinds of work took root during those months when building was impractical. The Community never lived permanently on the island, although many visitors still expect to find community members in residence there. The mainland work was *and is* a vibrant focus for the commitments of a growing Community.

> It was Friday lunch, a time for staff to relax together and eat up leftovers from recent meals at the centres. At the MacLeod Centre, we had just said goodbye to a group of refugees and community workers who spent the week with us. It had been a moving week. One of the families was called back early to face a hearing on their right to remain in Britain. When I said goodbye to them at the ferry, they embraced me with tears in their eyes. "This is the first time we felt welcome since we arrived in Britain," they told me. Humbling words to pass along to my colleagues on staff.
>
> At the lunch table, I was joined by a young man volunteering with us for a few weeks. Normally a cheerful lad with a scheme or two up his sleeve, he looked solemn. "Do you ken what those people have been through, Nancy? It's just nae fair." He had been deeply moved by what he'd heard from our guests.
>
> I reflected on the power at work among us. This young man had come to get his life straightened out. He'd had a brush with the law. Someone in the Community's network thought time on Iona would help him make a fresh start. In lots of ways, he hadn't had a fair chance, either. Yet here he was, marvelling at the courage of refugees also trying to make a fresh start. Their stories lay beyond anything he could imagine, just as his story lay beyond mine.

Inapprehensible, we know you, Christ beside us. George MacLeod's prayer insists that we take an honest look at the neighbours and strangers God puts beside us – on Iona and beyond. The Community draws such people who otherwise might never meet into moments where love and courage make new beginnings possible. The Community's concerns have included an important focus on young people for many years. George MacLeod pioneered opportunities for young men who had been in custody to spend time at Camas, the Community's wilderness adventure centre on the Isle of Mull. Camas continues its creative work with groups of young people, many facing difficult situations, offering challenges that call the best of their potential forward. At events for young people on Iona, economic and social boundaries often come down when young people look beyond their own neighbourhoods to encounter a larger world. This is the instinct that guides so much of the Iona Community's work. God works with us *in community* in transforming ways, drawing us beyond private interest and personal need, to discover who we can be and what we can offer to the world together.

To live together in unity

The Iona Community has grown and changed over nearly 70 years now. The membership is a dispersed network spread throughout the United Kingdom, with a small number of members found in countries around the world. A mix of women and men from many different churches and personal backgrounds, members share certain commitments that shape their daily lives. When members undertake to join the Community (a two-year process of participation and reflection), they take up a rule of life that has developed over the years into a five-fold practice. That rule commits members to daily prayer and Bible reading, local involvement in work for justice and peace, accounting to each other for the use of one's money and one's time, and membership in a family group. The family group becomes the local expression of the Community through which members hold each other accountable for living out the rule. Members are invited to recommit themselves annually, for the rule takes energy and intention. Each year I spent on Iona, I had the opportunity to meet members of the Community. I was deeply impressed by the range of activities in which they become involved in their home communities. Their contributions to deepening community life extend beyond the Iona Community itself into local neighbourhoods and churches as well as larger networks, both national and international. The Community also maintains a global network of associates and friends who support its work and its vision in a variety of ways.

People often assumed that as a member of the Community's staff and one of the wardens, I was also a Community member. Actually, only a few Community members are to be found among the island's staff from year to year. Still, resident staff, whatever our background, are in sympathy with many of the Community's concerns, which are emphasized in prayer and practice at the centres. The Community's commitments shape life at the island centres as staff and guests explore what it means to live together in unity – not an easy goal on many occasions!

> What a week! A virus was sweeping through the staff at both centres, a side effect of sharing the common life! Each day, it seemed, someone else was stricken with flu. Then, one of our program leaders phoned. A family emergency. Another gap to be filled that week. As I sat in my office, madly brainstorming program ideas, I was keenly aware that some of our guests might find their expectations for this visit to Iona unfulfilled.
>
> Soon I felt like a fish out of water. Although I had led workshops in Canada on the theme for the week, my program sessions just didn't go the way I imagined. Participants had very different expectations of the theme and I didn't seem to be able to read those expectations very effectively. Some of the evaluations stung.
>
> As we gathered at the ferry to say goodbye, I was glad the week was ending. Then one of the guests approached me, a piece of paper in her hand. "I know it's been a hard week," she said. "I want you to read this. It's a page from my journal. This has been an important week for me."
>
> The page recounted how deeply she identified with a biblical exercise we'd tried, one I thought hadn't connected with participants very well. God's healing power had touched her in a fresh way. No week on Iona is exactly what we expect, but God works within it and within us, thank goodness.

To describe a week spent as a guest at one of the centres would take more than a few paragraphs. Each week is filled with unique moments: some satisfying, some stressful. However, worship provides both continuity and creativity every week, whether you stay at the Abbey, the MacLeod Centre or elsewhere on the island. Because of the framework worship provides, I want to outline the series of services that form a typical week at the Abbey. This will help you place the material in this collection in its larger context – and perhaps imagine yourself there in the Abbey with us. You may also want to have a look at one of the various Worship Books developed for Iona Abbey over the years. Community members and island staff have collaborated to prepare resources for use in the Abbey. These books have become valued friends of those who lead worship in other settings. Each edition of an Iona Worship Book reflects the framework of daily life during a certain era on the island, as does my description here. I was involved on Iona from 2001 until 2004, a period when guest arrivals were timed for Saturday afternoons, with departures on the following Friday morning. Within that space of time, worship flowed in the pattern described below.

On Saturday evening, a service of welcome completes what for most guests has been at least one long day's travel, maybe more. Offering hospitality to friend and stranger is a central biblical commitment that is also foundational to the vision of time spent at the island centres. This first service in the cycle of a visit encourages people to reach out and say hello to each other, something we'll do many times in the days to follow. People are usually invited to talk in church, a hard thing for some folks to do, given the habits of a lifetime. This will be just the first opportunity among many in which we try on new ways of participating in worship, recognizing that we all bring something to share in worship – ourselves!

The Sunday morning service follows an order for the celebration of communion similar to liturgies in many Western Christian traditions. We are taught some easy-to-sing responses, creating wonderful harmonies as we are fed by God's Word and at God's Table. The songs will likely be a mix of old and new, drawing on the well of Iona Community music to help us sing with rhythm and relevance. Words spoken and sung in the Abbey are often inspiring, striking a fresh chord of recognition and response for many worshippers. However, Sunday evening leaves words behind. We gather in quiet for a lengthy time of silence, a chance to release to God the tensions of arriving and settling in and to savour the depth of God's presence.

Weekday mornings, worship follows a daily office, similar in form to the prayers said by Iona Community members wherever in the world they may be. The use of a morning office for daily prayer is well known throughout many Christian traditions. It echoes back to Columban and Benedictine practices of praying at regular intervals throughout the day, following a discipline of Bible readings and established themes for prayer. The Iona service includes a psalm and another passage of Scripture assigned for the day. Over the cycle of each month, every member of the Iona Community and every country in the world will be prayed for by name. Other concerns from the daily news are held before God alongside the ongoing work of the Community. My colleague John Bell from the Community once described using the morning office as "rehearsing" the commitments of our faith for the day ahead. I found his insight very helpful. I came to know the morning office by heart, but it was never a matter of saying it by rote. It became the solid framework for whatever surprises or challenges a day on Iona might hold. In three years, there were plenty of both!

For the mid-part of the season, afternoon prayers for justice and peace are said in the Abbey, upholding the kinds of concerns that are central to the rule of the Iona Community. These services are brief – only ten or fifteen minutes long – and are intended to include some of the many day visitors to the Abbey in an act of worship. The gathered numbers range widely, depending on bus schedules and the weather! In their own small way, these services lift up a wide variety of global situations in reflection and prayer with mustard seed faithfulness. Prayer and action are a deep part of each another in the spirituality rooted on Iona.

Evening worship at the Abbey brings variety and creativity to offer to God, and moves worshippers through a series of themes central to the Gospel week by week.

— On Mondays, the service focuses on a justice and peace concern. Social analysis joins biblical witness to call us to move, to change. We often move around the Abbey physically at some point in this service, symbolizing our hope for change within our own lives and within God's world.

— On Tuesdays, a service of prayers for healing provides the opportunity to receive prayer and the laying on of hands. This tradition is as deeply rooted in the history of the Iona Community as are prayers for justice and peace. The service is laid out very simply and includes prayer for people and situations drawn to the Community's attention through its worldwide prayer network, The Iona Prayer Circle.

— Wednesday evening highlights our commitment to Jesus Christ. This service is often planned and led by guests for the week. It will likely include a symbolic action, a gesture or movement to help us express our desire to follow Christ tangibly.

— Thursday is the final evening for guests to gather before catching the Friday morning ferry. Many Thursdays, we share communion in a style different from Sunday morning. Having drawn closer to each other over the preceding days, we draw closer around the table in thanksgiving for what God has given us in Christ and in each other. Some Thursdays, an Agape service will be held instead of communion, maintaining table fellowship through another ancient Christian pattern.

— Fridays, a day with fewer visitors around the island after our guests depart, the service is generally shorter and simpler than other evenings. It may draw on Celtic resources or lift up themes from creation, but then again the imaginations of the planners may introduce something entirely fresh for our reflection and prayer.

In this rich texture of worship, you will hear many different leaders. The Iona Community gathers its resident staff each year with a mix of new and continuing faces. About 25 people join the team, each agreeing to take an active part leading worship as well as attending regularly. Most staff members are not ministers or priests. They come from a fascinating variety of backgrounds to take up the diverse tasks involved in running the Community's centres. Some will lead their first service ever in the Abbey: no small task! The resident staff is joined by a constantly evolving group of volunteers who provide essential work to run the centres. Volunteers range upward in age from eighteen and come from around the world for six to sixteen weeks. Guests at the Abbey and the MacLeod Centre account for nearly a hundred people each week when both centres are full. Any one of these people could share in leading some part of a service.

It was Youth Clubs week at the MacLeod Centre, full of energy as young people between the ages of eleven and fourteen gathered for recreation and adventure (an adult's way of putting it, to be sure!). Nights ran later than usual and emotions were a little frayed. At the Wednesday morning staff meeting, I learned that the person who was planning the evening service was sick in bed. Guests often plan this service, so I offered to co-ordinate a team of young people to put a service together for that evening. Nothing like a deadline to insist on some creativity!

It was 10 a.m. when I shared this "opportunity" with the youth. Some of them were just barely awake. Seven young people volunteered to plan with me. Our chosen theme: Jesus' commitment to his friends. We spent the morning improvising drama, sorting out parts, picking songs and prayers. Other young people – and a few willing leaders – braided friendship bracelets. We figured we'd need 200 to have enough. Would it all come together in time? The bracelet factory continued all afternoon.

Rehearsal was a bit shaky. My ushers came late, still tying off a bracelet or two. There were nervous jitters as readers practised their lines. Too soon, people started to drift in the door. But I needn't have worried. The readers were fantastic. Clear, caring, focused. People laughed at the right moments. The words of a pop song played on a CD were a bit hard to hear, but the kids sang along in appreciation. Then we lined up to receive our friendship bracelets.

When it was my turn, I held out my hand, thinking one of the lads would drop a bracelet on my palm. But he took my wrist gently and tied on the bracelet, fingers intent on securing the knot. I looked at him in wonder. How many times had I cautioned him that week, asked him to stop this or try that? I looked at him and he smiled. Friends in Christ.

The Iona Community promotes broad participation when God's people gather. Giving volunteers and guests an opportunity to take part in a service was a particular joy for me. I saw many people blossom with new-found confidence. This collection features resources with parts for various voices, a strategy of outreach and encouragement to help new worship leaders uncover their gifts. Sharing leadership is also a way of painting with invisible colours – the colours created by age, gender and generation; by accent, sign and gesture; by ethnic roots and cultural milieu – all colours on God's palette.

On our heads and our houses

Many visitors are drawn to Iona in their search for Celtic spirituality these days. What they seek includes poetic appreciation for the wonder of creation and the blessings of the earth. Whenever conversation about such things took a rather romantic turn at the MacLeod Centre, my inner imp would chuckle. I'd recommend such seekers return in January, if the ferries were running.

> I arrived on Iona on a bone-chilling day in late January. A few days later, hurricane-force winds whipped around us. The ferry across the sound of Iona sensibly stayed in its shelter, but island life continued as normal – at least until the power went out. I ventured outside, thinking that as a Canadian, I had seen the wind. But that wind flipped me around and tossed me against a gate without a thought. When I saw a roof slate fly past, I reconsidered my courage.
> That night around nine o'clock, the wind dropped suddenly. Again I made my way outdoors, enjoying the subtle glow from coal fires and candlelight reflected in still-darkened windows. The moon was full, its trail of light glistening on the water. The air was calm but I could hear a constant roar, as if the wind still echoed in my head. It was the voice of the sea. In the moonlight, I stared at the water in wonderment. The sea was charged with energy. Waves galloped down the sound, racing against each other. In the brilliant moonlight, the crest of each

wave shimmered like the mane of a wild horse celebrating its freedom. Such power. Such threat. Such beauty. Such grace.

Celtic Christian prayer often celebrates the voice of creation praising God, pouring out blessing and deep peace. I felt a deep peace that night, peace born in awe of a day when my own strength failed in the wind. Iona's beauty is captivating – breathtaking colours of sea and sky; lacy foam dancing on the water as waves crash against rugged ancient rock; deep green hillsides laughing with brazen daffodils; the subtleties of heather skirting the bogs that lie in wait to capture another careless boot! In its small cradle, Iona embraces so much precious life. The world recites its own poetry before our eyes. We cannot help but wonder at the holy imagination that drew together such detail.

Yet, three winters on Iona taught me respectful humility in the face of storm-force winds and waves that crash not just on the shore but against the doorways along the village street. When the north wind rattled our bones as well as our windows, I marvelled at the faithfulness of monks hunkered down in their cells centuries earlier. I came to Iona not knowing much about the history of Celtic peoples. Oh, I had my share of "Celtic" prayer books filled with curling script and dragon-like doodles. However, it was the collections from the workaday world of Celtic family life that always attracted me. A whole day was wrapped in prayer, from getting dressed and setting the fire through daily chores – churning the butter, tending the herd – to nighttime blessings. No act was too small to be offered to God. Winters on Iona showed me how God's power and providence were needed to accomplish both dangerous and routine tasks on Hebridean crofts in years past. Danger is not very far away for those who live beside the sea today, as the islanders of Iona can testify.

As part of my teaching on Iona, I had to dig into Celtic Christian history, to study its patterns and details. Through our programs, I met several dedicated scholars of Celtic studies who helped me grapple with the differences in perspectives that mark this field. (Their books are noted in the bibliography at the end of this book.) I also recognized among members of the Iona Community a certain frustration with the search for "Celtic spirituality" that so often turns people inward, away from the need of neighbour and stranger. Such a turn is hardly true to Celtic Christian instinct. What *is* true is a generosity in heart and kind that reaches out in willing welcome to those in need, not stopping to count the cost. In workshops on Celtic heritage, I tried to honour the Iona Community's concern for the world in its brokenness as well as its beauty. Celtic Christian prayer in its full range can lead us beyond concern for our own thirsty souls to examine relationships and commitments in need of repair. God is surely to be encountered in the world and its wild wonder. But God's love can be as fierce as a gale when it spins us around and confronts us with our vulnerability and our arrogance, too.

As I sorted through this collection, looking for threads that would weave my reflections together, I recognized several themes that recurred in those workshops about Celtic spirituality. Of course, a small collection of occasional reflections like this will not provide a complete map of the Celtic Christian landscape. However, I hope that these resources will invite readers into the kind of conversations with Celtic heritage that occur within the Iona Community. These conversations hunt for the wisdom and the challenge in both scripture and tradition, listening for the forgotten note as well as the familiar cadence, always alert to deeper needs that clamour around and within us. I believe our explorations into spirituality, whatever path we take, ought never to expect that the way will be smooth. There will always be questions that urge us to open our eyes and take a fresh look.

God in Community, holy and one

"Unknowable, we know you, Christ beside us," prayed George MacLeod. I had been a professor of theology for ten years before I moved to Iona. Theologians are legendary for speaking of Christ in language nobody else can understand. At the MacLeod Centre where I came

to work, however, no theological jargon would do! There I met an incredible mix of people whose life circumstances varied as richly as their accents. As we traded stories around meal tables and did dishes together, I was often challenged to express my faith simply and directly to people who finally felt free enough to put a burning question into words. Away from my familiar classroom, surrounded by people from so many different situations, I couldn't rely on common assumptions or common vocabulary. I had to speak in everyday language. Soon I found that the conversational approach I needed at the centre was also welcome in worship. I began to rethink how to offer the fruit of my theological research as signposts for others who were travelling very different paths, to help them explore their own significant questions about God and God's potential for their lives.

Worship shared in the Abbey with such diverse and ever-changing congregations became a great adventure. This book gathers up the best of these adventures. You will find all kinds of material prepared for very different occasions. There are a few Sunday sermons. Many more take the shape of dialogues, dramas and stories. There is a bit of poetry, too. Each one was created with an eye for our guests on that particular occasion. At the MacLeod Centre, young people and school groups often joined the families and parish groups who regularly seek out time on Iona. The "Mac," as it is known affectionately, is also fitted with features to make it more accessible and welcoming for guests with disabilities. In our midst, quite likely you'd find a few international guests for whom English was not a first language, too. When I was planning worship, I would have this "cloud of witnesses" in mind. How could the words and actions, the songs and the silences of worship be accessible and welcoming for all participants? The Iona Community has developed a style of worship that is very honest in its praise and prayer. Therefore, I aimed to build services around honest questions, using straightforward language and true stories to acknowledge both the playful and painful sides of life. I tried to tell stories simply, leaving out certain details to protect the identities of individuals I encountered over the years. I wanted to show respect and affection for these lives that taught me something significant about God's presence and opened my eyes to my own shortcomings. If you recognize your life in one of my vignettes, know that I have come to a fuller appreciation of God's ways with us through you.

I made my choices of which items to include in this book based on feedback from a variety of participants. Often, someone would ask how I came up with an idea, a story or a design. This is a good question for a preacher and worship leader to consider. Part of preparing for worship involves hard work – studying, researching, thinking things through; imagining how time and space, words and silence, music and movement interact. But part of preparing for worship always depends on God. As I worked on this collection of resources, I had to think about how I recognize the work of the Holy Spirit – in the niggling thought that won't let go, the surprising insight, the fitting comment or the memory that suddenly leaps up to lead me in an entirely new direction. So many times I abandoned an early plan to follow the Spirit's insistence. In my recollections, however, I have also been humbled by what someone else experienced in a service, something I'd never even considered. I believe God honours the discipline that goes into preparing for worship but God will never be limited by the preacher's intention or imagination!

This collection can be sampled in several ways. Readers who enjoy exploring Scripture are invited to use this book for personal reflection. At the beginning of each item, I mention the Scripture I used as my source. You may want to read the passage before you look at my reflection. (When Scripture readings are worked into the text of a dialogue, I have quoted *The New Revised Standard Version*, which is the version of the Bible provided in the seats in the Abbey.) Enter into the design as much as you can; pause when silence is indicated; use the words of the suggested chants as a prayer refrain on your own. This is not a book intended to be read at one sitting. Each piece can be savoured in prayer or meditation as an act of worship.

To introduce each item, I have briefly described the situation or the people who were on my mind as I wrote. These companions will be reading over your shoulder, so remember you're not alone! If you are a worship leader or preacher yourself, you may find it helpful to think over how different people in your own community might respond to a design or a theme. You may find a resource you can borrow or an idea to adapt for your own situation. I hope so! Although each item was designed with Iona Abbey in mind, many of the approaches can be adapted for other worship spaces. For those on the hunt for some inspiration, I offer a Scripture index identifying the various biblical texts I used in my reflections. I have also identified when these Scripture texts occur in *The Revised Common Lectionary*, so that preachers who follow those assigned readings for the Christian year can check to see if there are any resources on a lectionary reading. (Please note, however, that this collection is not intended as a lectionary resource, given that I preached on Sundays only four or five times each year. Other services were designed thematically, not necessarily with the Christian year in mind.)

After each reflection, I've developed a section to describe how I came up with an idea and the kinds of choices I considered in shaping the service. Where I received insights after a service from participants, I've shared those, too. Here we are reading between the lines at Iona Abbey. As you read between the lines, think about your creative process and the ways in which God's Spirit works with you when you are immersed in worship planning. By thinking about how I select stories and place symbols in worship, I've become more aware about the choices I face as a leader. I'm learning when to resist my own preferences for the sake of those who will gather with me and when to take a risk and trust what God will do. By reflecting on my approach to worship design and the questions I struggle with, I hope that other worship leaders will consider how they make choices on behalf of those who gather with them in Jesus' name.

The everlasting God shield you

When I was appointed Deputy Warden of Iona Abbey, someone sent me a prayer written by Peter Millar, a former Warden:

> Lord of every pilgrim heart, bless our journeys on these roads we never planned to take, but through your surprising wisdom discovered we were on....

I went to Iona as a short-term volunteer and ended up coming back for three more years. Those years opened my eyes to Christ's invisible presence and the very visible gifts and needs that draw alongside us on the road in the people we meet. Pilgrimage is a journey we take for God's purposes – purposes that are seldom clear when we set out and will be rewritten as we go. I invite readers to enter this collection as pilgrims: reading, singing, praying through the pages as we would if we were walking together on the Iona pilgrimage. I hope what you see will invite you to wonder – about God, about your faith, about your community, about the next step you take.

The reflections that follow are gathered into seven sections. Each section begins with a short comment that links an aspect of Celtic Christian faith to some of the concerns and commitments of the Iona Community. As I laid out this pattern, however, I recognized that one major theme in Celtic Christian faith does not emerge at all, one that is very important to me: The Trinity. Many years ago, during early feminist debates about the traditional male symbols for the Trinity – Father, Son and Holy Spirit – I came across a collection of Celtic prayers. In its pages, the traditional Trinitarian names were used often. Yet woven around the male titles were other expressions of "three in one" and "one in three." The Celts could celebrate their Trinitarian faith in symbols from the natural world and in the intricacies of geometric pattern. There was unity and diversity as these prayers confessed faith in God the Trinity, whose mystery entwines our lives as creatively as Celtic knot work. With my Celtic forebears, I recovered my sense that God's mystery can never be fully expressed in language, either traditional or contemporary. Yet even in our homespun words, God's Word will address us face to face. So may I offer these resources to you

> In the name of the one true and Triune God:
> Source of Life and Love
> Christ of Tears and Laughter
> Spirit of Power and Promise
> In whom we live and move and have our being
> this day, every day and in that Day to come.

1

The Fierce Beauty of God

The beauty of Iona astonished me again and again. On a sunny summer day, the sea's deep turquoise laps against white sand beaches and brooding black rock formations. In winter, the sun drops in for a few blessed hours, offering fragile light that plays with shadows on surrounding cliffs from its vantage point far to the south. The sky changes with the wind, sometimes moment by moment. Rainbows smile across the hills to gladden the hearts of rain-soaked visitors. Just a glimpse can transform the other reality of Iona – galloping wind, leaden skies and water driven into the pores of your skin. Marvel at the sheep whose sweaters – or jumpers, as they are called there – soak it all in.

The experience of the wild wonder of Iona offers many images to evoke our praise of God, as you will find in this section. Celtic Christian tradition draws on the instinct of the psalms to appreciate all of nature responding to God's creative power. Yet it is hard to convey the sound effects that could accompany any one of my reflections to the reader who has never experienced a gale-force wind in the Hebrides. When a wind is howling, the Abbey magnifies its ferocious voice and rain adds its insistent rhythms to our singing. Then there are the days when it is so cold, wearing five layers is not enough for bodily comfort. Those days when nature's fierce power seemed unrelenting, even overwhelming, I pondered the tenacity of those monks who served with Columba when the north wind was blowing. How did they hold on to these blessed rocks in their wooden huts without the benefits of electric heaters and the miraculous waterproof fabrics of our generation? Their faithfulness to God's purposes humbled me whenever I felt like grumbling about the weather in Scotland.

The longer I lived on the rugged and resolute landscape of Iona, the more I reflected on God's ferocious nature, which insists we pay attention to what is damaged and desperate around us as well as within us. George MacLeod provoked people to open their eyes and recognize the heartache around them. To be nourished by the beauty of creation is not an end in itself. It is a source of strength and connection to propel us into life's ugly challenges, sure that God's Spirit is there with the same breathtaking, eye-opening force we have felt looking on to Iona's turquoise sea. In the Abbey, we drew from Celtic Christian imagery not merely to satisfy poetic sensibilities but to link us with the world in all its fullness: to recognize God's presence and power beyond the arenas of human control. I hope you will sense the fierce beauty of God as you read these reflections. The first was prepared shortly after Pentecost, the holy day that marked Columba's death on Iona in 597. The second explores Psalm 139, one of the biblical texts so beloved by Columban monks. For the final piece, imagine the depths of a starry winter night and listen to what the stars can see.

Born again?

This dialogue was constructed for four voices, drawing on readings from John 3.1-10 and 2 Corinthians 5.16-18. Written just after the celebration of Pentecost, it explores the image found in John's story using my encounters with wind on Iona to provoke my listeners' sense of how God's Spirit works with us. The chants interspersed throughout the dialogue were sung by the whole congregation. The music provided is taken from *Come All You People*, edited by John L. Bell, © 1995 Wild Goose Resource Group, Wild Goose Publications, Glasgow. Texts are supplied here so that you can pause and use the words to reflect on your own experience for a moment before reading further. If you know the chants, you might want to hum them over – or sing them out loud!

Voice One:

Now a Pharisee named Nicodemus came to Jesus by night and said to him:

Rabbi, we know that you are a teacher who has come from God;

for no one can do the signs that you do apart from the presence of God.

Voice Two:

And Jesus said, Very truly, I tell you,

no one can see the kingdom of God without being born from above.

Voice Three:

From now on, therefore, we regard no one from a human point of view.

Even though we once knew Christ from a human point of view,

we know him no longer in that way.

If anyone is in Christ, there is a new creation.

Refrain #1

Take, O take me as I am;___ sum - mon out what I shall be;___

set your seal up - on my heart and live in me.___

Voice Two:

No one can see the kingdom of God without being born again.

Voice One:

Nicodemus said to Jesus, How can anyone be born after having grown old?

Can one enter a second time into the mother's womb and be born again?

Voice Four:

I'm with Nicodemus.

Jesus' riddles seem too clever by half.

He chose a word that has two meanings

and managed to divide Christians across the centuries.

Voice Two:

No one can see the kingdom of God

without being born *from above*.

Voice One:
Without being born *again*.

(then in rapid succession)

Voice Two: Born from above.
Voice One: Born again.
Voice Two: Born from above.
Voice One: Born again.

Voice Four:
Poor Nicodemus stepped into the bog of Jesus' playfulness
and sank up to his knees.
How can anyone be born after having grown old?
Please, Jesus,
can you teach an old dog new tricks?
Is there some miracle of time travel
that would allow us to relive a time when things went badly and put
    things right?
Please, Jesus,
could you wind back the clock
and let us enjoy the days of childhood when we *thought* we were
    bored?
Or give us a chance to go back
and take the other turn in the road;
turn the other cheek;
turn over a new leaf
and see if we could get it right *this* time?
How can anyone be born after having grown old?

Voice Three:
From now on, we regard no one from a human point of view.
If anyone is in Christ, there is a new creation.

Refrain #1

Voice Two:

Jesus answered, Very truly, I tell you, no one can enter the kingdom
   of God
without being born of water and spirit. Do not be astonished that I
   said to you,
You must be born from above.

Voice Four:

But we *are* astonished.
Please, Jesus,
if you do not regard us from a human point of view,
do you mean that you never listened to our parents complain about
   us?
When other children teased us?
Did you not hear our teachers criticize us?
That police officer pull us over?
That coach humiliate us?
That nosy neighbour talk about us behind our backs?
That boss, that parishioner, point out our shortcomings
day after day, week after week?
We *are* astonished
if everything that has diminished us,
if everyone who demeaned us,
if every failure,
every mistake,
every short coming,
every thing that keeps us lying awake at night
has not turned you away from us.
To be born from above –
Is this to live with a reputation created by someone who loves us?
Is this to live with all our faults and frailties and yet to matter
in the great scheme of things?

Voice Three:

If anyone is in Christ, there is a new creation.

Refrain #*1*

Voice Two:

Do not be astonished that I said to you, You must be born from
    above.

The wind blows where it chooses, and you hear the sound of it,

but you do not know where it comes from or where it goes.

So it is with everyone who is born of the Spirit.

Voice Four:

Please, Jesus, another riddle?

We hear the sound of the wind day after day on this exposed island.

It can mess up our plans for the day.

It can cut us off from other people and places.

We marvel at its force.

We curse its relentless presence.

Are you like the wind, O God –

in our face;

changing our plans;

directing us in a way we didn't choose?

Relentlessly present;

resisting our excuses;

awakening us with a force beyond our control?

Could this be love:

in our face;

changing our plans;

directing us in a way we didn't choose?

Relentlessly present;

resisting our excuses;

awakening us with a force beyond our control?

Voice Three:

If anyone is in Christ, there is a new creation.
Everything old has passed away;
see, everything has become new!

Refrain #2

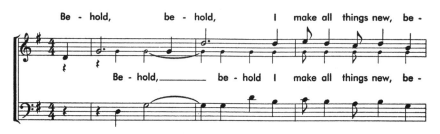

Voice One:
Nicodemus said to him, How can these things be?

Voice Four:
Nicodemus, don't you get it yet?
Feeling old and used up;
feeling young and pointless;
feeling caught in the middle;
insignificant;
unworthy;
unloved;
unsure;
the wind of the Spirit rattles through our windows
and our bones,
our memories
and appointment books
to blow away the debris that clutters our lives,
that fills our hearts with pain or anxiety.
The wind of the Spirit pushes a fresh wave of God's energy
against the rock of our self-understanding
to wash away feelings that cling to us like old seaweed.
The wind of the Spirit insists that a new direction *is* possible for us
because Christ will take away the burdens others have packed for us
    to carry.
Christ looks on us with the tender smile we reserve for a newborn
    baby.
Christ looks on us and sees what we can yet become.
Christ gives us new eyes for seeing –
to see a new possibility for our lives.
And to see in each other what we can yet become together
blessed and blown by the Spirit.

Voice Three:
All this is from God,
who reconciled us to himself through Christ,

and has given us the ministry of reconciliation.
Everything old has passed away;
see, everything has become new!

Refrain #2

Reading between the lines

Born again. A phrase that can provoke strong reactions. Where I grew
up, some people used the phrase "born-again Christian" to separate
the wheat from the chaff, the true believers from mere pretenders. As
a child baptized as an infant, raised to attend church regularly, I was
surprised to learn from such folks that I was a pretender to the faith,
unable to name a time and place when I had been "saved." Much
later, as a minister, I met a parishioner who told me if I preached on
the "born again" text in John, he'd leave the church. He was tired of
being judged, he said.

I remember quite clearly the day we studied the "born again" text
from John 3 in New Testament class. My professor, a scholar of Greek
language, pointed out with some satisfaction that the Greek words
usually translated "born again" should be translated "born from above."
My Presbyterian classmates and I nodded. Of course. This translation
solved the problem. Born from above, not born again. "Born-again
Christians" ought to study more Greek! But in my heart of hearts, the
new translation didn't help very much. I was as puzzled as Nicodemus.
What did it mean to be "born from above"?

Years later, having struggled as a preacher to appreciate the beautiful
and complex stories of John's Gospel, I began to see something new in
this story. Jesus says, "Unless you are born again/from above, you will
not *see* the kingdom of God." The Greek verbs helped me recognize the
playfulness in this story. Many of the verbs for "knowing" in this text
are verbs of "seeing," just like those times we understand something
and say "I see." Jesus invites Nicodemus to look at the world with new
eyes, like a newborn does. Jesus offers him a new perspective on life,

as if he's standing in a new place and looking at familiar things "from above." I suddenly saw that the slippery words to translate, born again or born from, create a deliberate double entendre. We are not supposed to choose one or the other as correct. Like Nicodemus, we are supposed to be puzzled. For in working out the puzzle with Jesus, we are given a new angle on familiar things. We are given a second chance to see ourselves, to see the world, and to see God's unfolding purposes within and beyond us all. The wind is our clue. We can't actually see it, but we can see its force. We can't actually see the moment God moves within someone's life, but we will see the changes that love can work.

I wrote the dialogue as a deliberately playful exploration of this discovery. Very few of the guests I met on Iona described themselves as "born again" Christians. Many more would squirm a bit at the term. Yet all of us, whatever our assumptions about the phrase, can appreciate the need for a second chance after we've done something we regret. It is good news that God's grace allows us to make a fresh start. I wanted people to grasp this common truth, which is more important than choosing between divisive translations. But rather than load people with too many bits of New Testament Greek, I decided to find a text to complement John's story with a bolder assertion about seeing things anew according to God's grace. The text from 2 Corinthians 5, with its gospel promise that "From now one we regard no one from a human point of view," immediately came to mind. Pretty well everyone I know has encountered a hurtful, limiting human point of view on their lives, their value, their actions or ability. So Paul's affirmation is good news! I think it is the same good news that John has woven into his story of Nicodemus and Jesus. If anyone is in Christ, there is a new creation. Born again or born from above, it doesn't matter. Behold, the new has come. Thanks be to God.

Still, this good news is something many Christian people find it easier to believe on behalf of others than for themselves. Hurtful human points of view often scar us deeply and limit our sense that God sees us with loving eyes: gives us – yes, us – the opportunity to become someone new.

Therefore, I chose two of the shorter songs for worship, composed by John Bell, to soak our lives in the gospel promise. The first chant, *Take, O take me as I am,* is a lovely, haunting plea that finishes with the hope that God's Spirit will live in us just as we are. Its melody gradually builds to a surge that can release a lingering fear or an old hurt deep within. The second chant is a more energetic proclamation of the promise in 2 Corinthians. Its words sing as from the lips of Jesus himself, assuring us that Christ can make us all new. Singing in response to the spoken promise deepens people's hold on the promise, I believe. Somewhere I read these words, attributed to the nineteenth-century theologian Friedrich Schleiermacher: "What the Word makes clear, music makes alive." The songs of my colleague John Bell so often exemplify this insight, as this service showed me.

This dialogue and reflection were written to lead us into an evening communion in the Abbey, where we sat around the table set down the centre aisle of the church. We continued to use the two chants within the communion liturgy. I can say that it was a powerful moment to break the bread and offer the loaf to people as they sang with joyful energy, *"Behold, I make all things new."* Many participants who spoke to me after the service found the collision of the two scripture texts helpful, even freeing. Singing these refrains within the celebration of communion gave them a deeper reverence when the familiar words were read:

This is my body broken for you. Take and eat.

This is not a human point of view. This is God's new creation, meant for us, already beginning in us, healing, renewing and making us whole through Christ the Way.

When God is with us

Here is a sermon based on Psalm 139 and Luke 6.27-8, 32, 36, preached in Iona Abbey one Sunday morning. The lessons are from the *Revised Common Lectionary* readings for that particular day of the year. It is the custom in the Abbey to read one or two of the designated lessons each Sunday. The Sunday liturgy includes the celebration of Holy Communion each week. For this service, I chose a musical setting of Psalm 139, written by Ian Pitt-Watson, from *The Church Hymnary* of the Church of Scotland, which we sang as the hymn before the sermon. The last verse of that hymn became the prayer that led us through this exploration of the psalm, inviting us to wonder about God's far-reaching presence and the intimacy with which God knows us. I hoped that singing this refrain would give us all a little time to face some of the things we like to avoid in our own lives and in our relationship with God. I also introduced comments from my research with children about their sense of who God is, in dialogue with lines from the psalm. I wanted listeners to recognize that the themes of Celtic Christian tradition, which frame my interpretation of the psalm, also find echoes in the instinctive wonder children bring to God's world.

Celtic spirituality.
Many folk come to Iona in search of something they identify with this
    term.
When I lead workshops on this theme, people talk about art –
Celtic interlace and knot work, carved crosses,
    illustrated manuscripts.
People talk about music –
haunting melodies or dancing tunes of flute and fiddle.
And very often, people mention God's presence in nature –
the mystery and wonder of the world
speaking of God's mystery and wonder.
To be sure, these features can be found in the faith of many Celtic
    cultures.
Prayers and poems gathered from the Scottish highlands
confess faith in God
whose power embraces us in the fierce beauty we see all around us
on this holy isle.

Voice One: Where can I flee from your spirit?
                Where can I flee from your presence?

Voice Two: If I take the wings of the morning
                And settle at the farthest limits of the sea,
                Even there your right hand shall hold me fast.

Many ancient peoples wondered at the presence of God
encountered in the depths of a starry night
and revealed in the colours of rock and the vast expanse of the sea.
No wonder the Celts had an affinity for the psalms of ancient Israel.
But others also wonder about God's presence around us.

Voice One: God is in the room with you but you can't see him.
                He's in *every* room.

Voice Two: Can astronauts see God or angels flying around?
                God will have to wear an air mask because there's no air
                in space.

Today's children give voice to that ancient sense of God's mysterious
    presence,
as near as this room and as far as the reaches of outer space.
When I interviewed children in Canada and here on Iona
about God,
I heard a very Celtic sense of God's presence.
Lorne, age 9, said to me quite confidently, "God watches over us."
But then he asked me whether God could see him
when he and his younger brother fought over their toys!
This is an important consideration,
whether we listen to this psalm as seekers after a Celtic sense of the
    world
or as children suddenly aware that God's amazing presence
means God is witness
to those moments when we'd like to give our little brother a shove.
There are three visions of God in Psalm 139,

and each contains a challenge for us.
When we marvel at the God of the cosmos,
do we hope that such a mysterious creator is *so* vast
as to let us off the hook for the way we behave?
Celtic Christians of ancient days would not allow us to neglect our neighbours
or mistreat our little brothers
without a sense of contrition before God, our Creator.

Voice One: You are acquainted with all my ways.

Voice Two: Even before a word is on my tongue,
                 O Lord, you know it completely.

Small wonder that confession of sin is also part of Celtic Christian prayer.
No solitary search for God's presence in the beauties of nature
lets us away with causing harm to neighbour or ignoring a stranger.
And so, as we sing with the psalmist, we invite God to examine our daily affairs:

Chant: *Search me, O God, search me and know my heart.*
            Try me, O God, my mind and spirit try;
            Keep me from any path that gives thee pain,
            And lead me in the everlasting way.

Natalie was walking to the north beach with me.
Suddenly she stopped and gestured at the sky.
"God isn't just up there, you know. He's down here with us. He's in my heart.
And your heart."
She paused and looked into the field. "He's in the sheep's heart."
As she looked at the ground, she nodded.
"And he's in the stone's heart, too."
Natalie hadn't read anything about Celtic spirituality.
She was just four years old that day.

But she certainly holds the second vision of God
common to both the Celts and the psalmist.

Voice One: You knit me together in my mother's womb.

Voice Two: I am fearfully and wonderfully made.

The psalmist paints such an intimate picture of God's connection
    with us.
Here is the tenderness we know
when we marvel at the perfection of a baby's fingers.
Here is Natalie's confidence that God knows her – and the sheep in
    the field –
from the inside out.
But the psalmist also recognizes:

Voice One: Such knowledge is too wonderful for me.

Too wonderful, perhaps,
for those of us who live uncomfortably in our bodies,
unsure about our shape and look;
tempted to quiet our self-doubts with comfort food or some other
    substance.
Such knowledge
that God has a concern for the intimate details of our physical life
gives me pause to think about my daily details.
Is the way I look after my health and well-being
as much a form of discipleship as coming to worship
or offering money to help those in need?
Is choosing a well-balanced diet and regular exercise
a spiritual discipline like prayer?
The psalmist asks God to search our hearts,
remembering that each of us is fearfully and wonderfully made.

Chant: *Search me, O God, search me and know my heart.*
          Try me, O God, my mind and spirit try;
          Keep me from any path that gives thee pain,
          And lead me in the everlasting way.

We haven't heard the third vision of God voiced by the psalmist.
The scholars who proposed the reading of Psalm 139 for this
    Sunday
carefully left out the messy bits.

Voice Two: O that you would kill the wicked, O God.
             Do I not hate those who hate you, O Lord?

Voice One: I hate them with perfect hatred.
             I count them my enemies.

Eek.
Such sentiments in Holy Scripture make us uncomfortable.
Yet we ignore them at our peril,
for they are our sentiments, too, at least from time to time.
Let us not forget that tradition suggests St. Columba's voyage to
    Iona
may well have been an act of penitence
for a bloody battle between royal households in Ireland
for which Columba was partly responsible.
Asking God to take vengeance on our enemies has long tempted people
    of faith.
Such sentiments fill our world these days,
when people of differing religious traditions point to people of *other*
    traditions
as enemies of God.
Sadly,
people are ready to kill those whom they name as God's enemies.
But listen to the voices of today's children.
Anna, age nine:

Voice Two: God wants us to forgive each other.
                If people never forgave each other, it'd be a cruel world.

Six-year-old Sandy:

Voice One: God has love for everyone in the world.
                He has the most love of all.
                I only have enough love for some people.

Sandy, with a child's honesty, has put her finger on the truth.
We cannot manage to love everybody on our own.
And so the words of Jesus stand as a constant challenge to us
just as they stood as a challenge to the psalmist's anger.

Voice Two: Love your enemies;
                do good to those who hate you.
                Bless those who curse you,
                pray for those who abuse you.

Voice One: If you love those who love you,
                what credit is that to you?
                Even sinners do the same.
                Be merciful, just as God is merciful.

Psalm 139 opens with amazing wonder
for God's creativity and inescapable purpose.
It paints tender images of God's intimate presence
with us from our vulnerable infant beginnings.
Its unsettling outburst of anger is hard to take.
But the *silence* of God's voice in this psalm
suggests to me that God rejects this cry for vengeance.
For God responds to human anger and outrage
with the challenging mercy of Jesus Christ.
Here is the challenge we must take up in the present moment.
Too many innocents are being lost or betrayed in campaigns of religious
    anger.

The psalmist asks God,

Voice One: Search me, O God, and know my heart.
Test me and know my thoughts.

Voice Two: See if there is any hurtful way in me
And lead me in the way everlasting.

The psalmist's anger is honest, to be sure,
but it is also hurtful.
The way everlasting is the way Jesus walked.
The way that resists – even rejects – retaliation.
The way that risks love for enemies.
His is the way of goodness and mercy for all God's children,
not just for some.

Chant: *Search me, O God, search me and know my heart.*
Try me, O God, my mind and spirit try;
Keep me from any path that gives thee pain,
And lead me in the everlasting way.

Reading between the lines

Psalm 139 is one of my favourite psalms. I love its immense vision of God's presence. When I left the west coast of Canada for the west coast of Scotland, settling "at the farthest limits of the sea" seemed an appropriate image for me. Whichever direction you look from Iona's shores, you can appreciate the expanse of the world that God embraces in all its colour and beauty. It is no wonder that the prayers of Celtic Christians, collected over many generations, convey the same appreciation of God's presence, read from the text of the natural world as well as the psalms. My work on Iona involved leading sessions on St. Columba and Celtic Christianity with guests at our centres. The more research I did for these discussions, however, the more strands of Christian tradition I had to weave together to create the full texture of the faith of Scottish Celts. This sermon attempted to draw some of those strands together.

Psalm 139 was the psalm assigned for the Sunday I preached, but only certain verses were proposed for reading. Four verses toward the end of the psalm, ranting against enemies, had been left out. This was no surprise. So often when we read psalms in church, we leave out the parts that disturb us. The same is true for some seekers after "Celtic spirituality" who visit Iona. They want a spirituality that fits an ideal – honouring the beauty and wonder of the natural world and, perhaps, affirming the goodness of human life. But confession of sin and responsibility for one's neighbour are very often missing from the attributes of Celtic faith named by participants in my workshops. Given that many of the themes of the psalm resonate profoundly with Celtic Christian piety, I thought the missing bits of the psalm might remind us of important realities we prefer to avoid in our spiritual searching.

As I wondered how to draw people into reflection on both the beauty and the challenge in the psalm, the voices of children came to mind. I interviewed many children in Canada and on Iona as part of a research project on children's questions about God. In that project, reported in my book *Growing up with God: Using Stories to Explore a Child's Life and Faith*, I was struck by children's honesty about the hard parts of their relationships. In our conversations, children often reflected on difficulties in friendships and in getting along at home. Sometimes they also puzzled about world situations and cruelty reported in the news. Their honesty and their expectation seemed to add an important voice to the dialogue between the psalm and its Celtic connections.

When I was working with the angry verses of the psalm, I was struck by the intensity of its emotion and parallels I was hearing all around me. In the United Kingdom, the so-called war on terror had ignited deep feelings against Muslims, who were being perceived in their neighbourhoods as a like-minded group bent on violence. They were easily identified as "enemies," at least by some. At the same time, people judged to be complicit with America's occupation of Iraq had become kidnap targets in that country, some beheaded by angry captors. Enemies targeted once more. The day after I wrote this sermon, a school in southern Russia was seized by terrorists, apparently as part of an ongoing ethnic and religious struggle in the area. A huge number of children who had gone to school for the first day of a new term became victims of vicious brutality. The words of the children I had chosen for the sermon rang out in the abbey in sad tribute to their innocence, lost to flames of adult anger. The killing of children is the kind of travesty that can surely ignite the outrage expressed by the psalmist. But if the world is ever to be a safer place for a new generation of children, we must take up the challenge in Jesus' teaching about enemies – long before another school comes under siege or another passenger plane becomes a deadly weapon.

It depends how you look at it

I wrote this dialogue for Christmas Day at the end of my first year on Iona. I had been inspired by the stars over the Hebrides night after night, drawn to the telescope owned by a colleague, to gaze into the depths of the galaxy. On Christmas morning at the Abbey, there is often a short service for families with children who have come away from their early morning Christmas merriment to glimpse God's purposes once again. Over the years, I have written many resources for the Christmas season to be used with children. I've given voice to sheep and cows and donkeys and camels, angels and shepherds, too. As I puzzled over what angle to take on the familiar story of the Christ child, my fascination with the stars lit up my imagination.

Morning Star (MS): AAAAAA – choooooo!

Evening Star (ES): Bless you. A little stardust in your nose?

MS: It must have been a bit of the tail of that comet that streaked past me 200 years ago.

ES: A bit of an ass-teroid, that one!

MS: Comet. Asteroid. It all depends how you look at it.

ES: Shooting star or meteor. It just depends.

MS: Like that baby the other morning.

ES: Oh yes, the wee one with that crowd of angels 2000 years ago.

MS: Give or take a few days. That's the one.

ES: The night he was born, there was a great crowd in the town. Not just angels. Travellers. Tramps. And shepherds, too. With quite a few sheep straggling along. You know how they'll follow their shepherd.

MS: Yes, they'll go anywhere for a good graze. But by the time we morning stars were watching, no one else was about. Just the mother and her baby. As far as I could see…

ES: Which is quite a few million light years…

MS: As far as I could see, his mother seemed a bit sad that morning. As she washed him with salt and water, I thought I saw a tear in her eye.

ES: Perhaps it was a tear of joy. To have her baby safe after such a long journey. It just depends how you look at that tear!

MS: Oh, yes. But mothers weep when they think of the hard times babies have to face growing up on that sorry planet Earth.

ES: That sorry planet Earth? My dear Morning Star, Earth is one of the most beautiful gems in that galaxy. Green and growing. Seas of crystal blue. Wisps of white cloud. It all depends how you see that planet.

MS: Oh, elegant Evening Star, you always see the beauty. You're remembering Earth the way God spun it from the vapours of her love and the dust of his desire. Billions of years ago. But today, we morning stars hear the earth groaning. And even yesterday, when that wee baby was born, there were people who were poor; people who were angry; people fighting each other. A sad place, this Earth.

ES: My dear despairing Morning Star, you have forgotten the days between yesterday and today, the days that wee baby touched the earth with love. It all depends what you remember. Remember how he loved the earth, walking the hills by himself? How he loved the sea, even when the wind and the waves were wild! Remember how he loved a good time with his friends, and how he smiled at those little children who used to get under his feet. People followed him like sheep follow a shepherd, sure he'd show them the safest path.

MS: Indeed, Evening Star, I remember. Stars are always watching. Whether people can see us or not. That wee baby, his eyes twinkled like stars. He was watching everything! And his smile seemed to light up that dark old shed where he was born. Maybe his mother knew he would have a good hard life because so many people watched him, just like we did.

ES: And they still do watch him, like we did. And it all depends what they see in him. Is he just another baby? Or is his new life a sign of new life for every dusty, crusty creature – even sneezing stars!

MS: (*Sniffs*) Is he a storyteller with a good line? Or is he God's Word acted out in a human life? It *does* depend on what you see in him.

ES: I see in him God's ancient light born to show people a new way through the darkness. Like a star, you might say. But we know – a star shines for a long time before people see the light.

MS: (*Nods*) I hear in him God's ancient song. Sometimes he's a love song to warm the heart of the universe. Sometimes he's a lament because God's heart is breaking for the pain and fear he touches on earth. It depends on what you hear in him.

ES: Morning Star!

MS: Evening Star!

MS and ES together: People wonder what we are!

ES: But we wonder, what do you see in this wee baby?

MS: We wonder, what do you hear in his life for your life?

ES: His light shines in your darkness, and the darkness shall not overcome it.

MS: His life is light for all people, full of grace and truth. Even for you.

MS and ES together: May his life be light for this world to warm your heart and guide your path – for all the light years to come!

Song: while participants move to pick up cut-out stars

A prayer:

Voice One: God of all time and space, God of the stars and the moon

Voice Two: God of miracle and manger, God of birthday candles and the Christ candle

Voice One: We pray that the worship we have shared this Christmas may lead us to act for goodness in the lives and places we touch. May the carols we have sung help others to sing, even in their sadness.

Voice Two: May the gifts we have given and gotten this Christmas teach us to be generous throughout the coming year. May the candles that cheer us this Christmas remind us that you intend no one to live in darkness.

Voice One: May the new people we have met this Christmas show us that you will meet us in both friend and stranger.

Voice Two: May the stories we've shared again this Christmas be good news of great joy to us and to all people.

Voice One: We remember before you with thanksgiving all the people and places, all the creatures and the features of this world that fill our hearts with gladness...

Voice Two: We remember before you with love and concern all the people and places, all the creatures and features of this world that face struggle or fear, sorrow or danger this day. Hold them in your love…

(*after 10 seconds*)

Voice One: Hear these prayers and all the silent prayers of our hearts, O God.

Voice Two: And cradle them and us in your holy wisdom for Christ's sake. Amen.

Reading between the lines

I was often overwhelmed by the night skies above the Hebrides, the islands off Scotland's west coast. Far away from city lights, we could see so many stars. The translucent path of the Milky Way flowed over our heads, drawing the eye across the galaxy. I spent my winter nights on Iona, star chart in hand, learning to identify constellations and calling the stars by name. My wonder was deepened when we took a telescope to the north end of this tiny island. To study the colours of a star's incredible combustion enhanced their elegant beauty twinkling in the deep velvet of night. Staring into the nebula in the belt of Orion, I marvelled that stars whose birth I was watching had been born millions of years before their infant light shimmered before my eyes.

As Christmas approached, it struck me that light from some of the stars born on the same night as Jesus would still be travelling toward us. Two thousand light years isn't all that far in galactic terms. We haven't seen the light of those stars yet! I began to consider how the stars might tell the story of Jesus' birth, given everything else they see. Many children are fascinated by stars and outer space, especially in a place like Iona with its vast twinkling canopy. Under the light of light years, I wanted to expand our sense of time and space to consider Jesus' significance for the mysterious depths of God's creation. As the conversation between the stars grew, I thought that the stars might help us hold the innocence of the cradle and the wisdom of the cross in dialogue – without making Christmas morning too solemn. And so the characters of the Morning Star and the Evening Star took shape, inspired by the words of the carol "O Little Town of Bethlehem" as well as Luke's story of the night Jesus was born.

I anticipated the presence of young children at worship on Christmas morning and considered the importance of visual symbols to help them listen. The two of us who gave voice to the stars stood about 10 metres apart, facing each other down the centre aisle of the abbey. We each held a powerful flashlight. When one of us was speaking, the other made us "twinkle" by playing the light over us. This seemed like a simple symbol to keep young children engaged in the conversation, for I knew that some lines would speak to adults and some would make the children laugh.

Following the dialogue, participants were invited to come and pick up a star cut out of shiny gold and silver wrapping paper. We sang a carol while people moved about the church. When we came to the prayer, most people held their own star, which fit easily in the palm of one hand. The stars offered young participants a tangible focus during the prayer as well as a symbol of the service to take home. The prayer was written to pick up some of the themes of the dialogue and connect them to our lives in concrete ways children could identify with.

After the service, one line was cited back to me, having caught the attention of a few adults. The Evening Star says, "But we know – a star shines for a long time before people see the light." This reality of stars helped a few people consider the ongoing mystery in Christ and its power to fascinate us again, even though we've known the story for a long time. The children were very interested in the flashlights after the service and wanted to try the twinkling technique. But they also carried away their stars, so I trust the Light will continue to shine on them.

2

Holy, Wholly Holy

A day at the island centres is framed with worship. At the end of the morning service, no one sits down to reflect privately. As the rubric from *The Iona Abbey Worship Book* states, "We remain standing to leave, the work of our day flowing directly from our worship." This current practice reflects a conviction of George MacLeod when he drew the first group of craftsmen and student ministers together in 1938. Worship enlivens us for our work, whatever that may be. When we return to worship later that evening or later in the week, we will bring our workday concerns with us and meet them again in worship – through engaging God's Word, in prayer that embraces the world, in song that energizes us for action.

The link between worship and workday is the pulse of spirituality within the Iona Community. For me, it is also a link with the Celtic Christian tradition of praying through each task of the day, encircling the whole day in the presence of God, committing each purpose to God. From this perspective, each day is wholly holy. Our focus on God is not reserved to a specific time on a specific day such as Sunday. We ask God to bless us in and through ordinary actions, not only those "holy acts" we associate with worship. In a sense, then, every action is a component of our worship, a thought with significant implications for how we do whatever we do. Remember we do *everything* before God.

Still, this all-pervading sense of God's claim on our lives is not easy to embrace. Those of us who lived at the Abbey year-round sometimes found that daily worship lost its wonder and took on the character of work. Wherever we work and worship, it is surely easier to confine our spiritual interest to those times when we feel ready for God than it is to open every aspect of our lives to God. A rule of life, whether from St. Columba, St. Benedict or the Iona Community, calls us back into community with worship as its heartbeat, especially during those times when our own strength or interest is ebbing with the tide.

In this section, I have included four reflections. The first explores a challenge for many people wherever we worship – Iona Abbey or local parish. What do we do when worship feels like going through the motions and not like a living encounter with God? The second piece was created during a Youth Festival on Iona and uses humour to engage young people in examining the daily challenges God presents to us in our relationships. The third item draws wisdom and wonder from an ordinary life and an extraordinary moment within it. Such a story invites us to consider how any life can contain amazing grace. Finally, there is a poem that formed the reflection during a service of prayers for healing. These Abbey services dare to lay the needs of the whole world before God, trusting that nothing in life or in death is beyond God's concern. Through both the challenges and the opportunities we face, God has a word and a way for us so that we may know our lives are wholly held by God.

Going through the motions

This sermon explores John 2.1-11, the story of Jesus turning water into wine to save a wedding from a crisis. On my mind were discussions we seemed to have every year among staff at a point when at least a few people found attending worship each day more of a burden than a gift. I was also struggling with a text that is often interpreted to present faith in Christ as an improvement on Jewish prayer and piety, an attitude that can contribute to Christian complicity in discrimination against Jewish people. Our heartfelt discussions suggested to me that an interpretation of this text ought to take into account what Christians themselves experience when something once fresh and provocative has become familiar and alienating.

What does your morning ritual look like?

What do you do almost automatically when you wake up?

I turn off the alarm…for the fourth time,

turn on the light, then the radio,

feed the cat,

put on the kettle,

and head for the bathroom.

Only once freshly brewed coffee is in my mug am I paying attention
     to the day.

I have to go through these motions to get my day started right.

Such daily rituals place us in the world.

They give us a kind of confidence to start the day.

Other familiar rituals help us develop responsibility and social grace.

Think how many rituals we teach our children:

brush your teeth, say please and thank you, hang up your coat, shut
     the fridge door.

On it goes.

The ritual motions of childhood shape us as adults

according to the customs of our culture.

But all these rituals are not to be confused with life at its fullest.

We want our children to do more than brush their teeth after every
    meal
and shut the fridge door every time.
Daily rituals simply prepare us to grow in the world and find our path
    forward.

John tells us the story of a very important ritual:
a wedding.
A wedding and all that goes into it
is preparation for the richer, though more complicated, experience of
    married life.
And at this wedding,
like many weddings I've conducted,
something unexpected takes place.
Now whenever something unexpected happens in a ritual,
when we're interrupted,
we have to stop and consider whether it matters to our more important
    purposes.
In a wedding, if the bridegroom gets the hiccups, for example,
we pause a minute and then keep going with the vows.
The vows will still hold.
But if someone stands up to object to the marriage for a good and
    serious reason,
the wedding will have to stop.
The future has to be sorted out, then and there.

John tells the story of Jesus at a wedding
when something unexpected happened
so that we can stop and consider *our* relationship with God.
The story is filled with symbols the prophets used:
Wedding feasts,
bridegrooms
and wine, lots of it,
are all symbols of our relationship with God.

God's love for us is as intimate and tender as bridegroom for bride;
life with God is intended to be as joyful as a wedding feast
and as enriching as faithful marriage.
But the wine runs out.
The feasting is in jeopardy.
And so water
usually reserved for ritual motions of hand-washing and prayer before
a meal
is put to new use.
That water becomes the wine of new life with Jesus' blessing.

Now sometimes this story is taken to be a contrast
between the prayerful rituals of faithful Jews
and the joyful celebrations of Jesus' followers.
Jews, this interpretation argues, were just going through the motions
of faith.
Followers of Jesus had discovered the good wine.
But I think this old interpretation misses the point.
Any religious ritual can lose its connection to God
when people feel like they are just going through familiar motions,
as we do to start our day.
If we asked people who *used to* come to church
why they don't come anymore,
many of them would say, in one way or another,
that they don't get anything out of worship.
Sunday morning ritual doesn't lead them into an encounter with
God
that they find fulfilling.

And so this story of a crisis at a wedding
is for anyone who has ever felt, even for a little while,
that we were just going through the motions when it came to our
faith.
If we've ever nodded off in a sermon,
stayed in bed on a rainy Sunday,

or lost heart or hope in God,
Jesus comes to the wedding in Cana
to wake us up by tossing his wine in our face.
180 gallons of it.
Jesus has arrived in the nick of time
to drench us in God's promise
that the good life is still waiting for us.
There is better wine in store than what we've tasted so far.
The cup of salvation is filled with abundant life,
if we will just allow ourselves to drink deeply of God's love.

This story is a challenging reminder
that our prayerful reflections,
our beautiful and dignified liturgies,
our familiar and steadying services –
all these are only preparations for the fullness of life.
And the fullness of life comes as a gift from Jesus Christ
to refresh our souls and make our hearts glad
so that we can live with commitment and purpose in God's world.
But how are we going to claim the gift Jesus brings?

In this story, Mary gives us a clue.
She looks for Jesus and tells him what's gone wrong.
Then she challenges him to do something
and she expects him to make a difference.
If we are to follow Mary's lead,
first we have to consider what's going right –
and what's going wrong –
in us and around us.
It's important to name before God in worship the situation as we know
    it.
Yet the situation will be a little different for each of us here
as well as for anyone we know who stayed home today.

For example,
some of us may be bothered by something we've done
or something that's been done to us.
We may be in a situation where we're carrying something too heavy
    to manage.
And we could use a little help to make a fresh start.
When we're bothered by regret or failure or wrongdoing,
Jesus draws for us the good wine of forgiveness,
the cup of freedom to try again.
And it does taste good to know that with God,
new things *are* possible
even for us.

But some of us are likely carrying on with a different burden,
faced by a different situation.
It could be sorrow too great to speak of,
disappointment that has shattered our hope,
or the nibbling fear that we don't matter.
For us, the cup of salvation is held by someone
who has walked through pain and betrayal by friends,
who has faced death itself,
to promise us that God's love will never let us go.
For us, Jesus draws the good wine of compassion.
And as we take the cup to sip,
he will sit with us
and hold us
until we can put the pieces of our life back in place;
until we can meet his tender smile with one of our own.
He's not in a rush.
He'll wait with us.

And surely, some of us look around and wonder, what's the point?
What are we supposed to do?
The world is confusing, worrying.
We may be angry

at the government,

at the Church,

at structures that get in the way of sharing the good life with all who
deserve it.

We may be angry at God, too,

because things seem to go from bad to worse.

When Jesus raises his cup for us, he's got a glint his eye.

He's daring us to take the cup,

and to share the cup.

He's calling us to act for what we believe in.

He's offering us the cup of justice and joy.

To take this cup is to join Christ's party

and share the cup with all who thirst for a better future.

The wedding at Cana points to God's promise of life in abundance,

life in which we discover again and again that God still has something
more,

something better to offer us,

no matter what our situation.

Life in Christ is always more than going through the motions.

Living with Christ is to drink deeply from the cup of salvation,

whatever situation we find ourselves in,

and to feel the warmth and energy of God's goodness deep in our
bones.

Jesus came to Cana as a sign

that life with God is a celebration of mercy and love;

it is a promise that fills us with hope and courage.

So for a moment

think about how you were feeling when you got out of bed,

while you were going through the motions of your morning.

Think about the last few days

or weeks

or years.

Be a little daring like Mary.

Offer your situation to Jesus.
Hold it up to him in your heart.
And believe that he is holding out his cup –
the cup of salvation –
with a gift that is meant for you.
Drink deeply of God's love and receive what you need,
whatever you need.
For God has more than enough love and life and laughter
to fill every thirsty soul.

Reading between the lines

Worship in Iona Abbey includes patterns and practices developed in many different Christian churches as well as the creative designs that grow out of the faith and insight of current staff and guests. Our morning services, Monday through Saturday, follow a daily office: that is, a simple service of prayer, song and Scripture reading laid out in a framework used day by day. Many Christians will be familiar with some form of daily prayer that follows a set pattern. Staff who serve at the island centres say the office day after day, week after week, month after month. For some, the regular rhythm of its words and the strength of its familiar pattern become a welcome foundation to the day in a context where many things change constantly. But for others, familiar words are too repetitive. They sometimes express a sense that these services feel like going through the motions. In our staff meetings, we often debated the value of structure and spontaneity as aspects of common worship – to no shared conclusion!

In light of these conversations, the traditional interpretation of John's story as portraying Jewish daily prayer rituals as less meaningful than "true" Christian worship no longer felt convincing. Daily ritual and repeated prayer can draw some people very close to God. From all the reading I'd done on Celtic Christian practice, I thought that Celtic patterns of household prayer said over the butter churn and the cow in the field held similar reverence for daily details as do Jewish customs of hand-washing and prayer before meals. Perhaps we had been too glib in projecting our own worship preferences into the interpretation of this story. On Iona I learned that a deeply meaningful practice for some could lose its significance to others. The story no longer seemed to be a critique or a rejection of a particular practice in Judaism. Its wisdom was as much for Christians who had lost their taste for the worship of God.

Now, weddings are rituals that many of us who preside learn to tolerate rather than enjoy because of all the demands and expectations that surround what ought to be a holy moment. Every minister I know has both funny and exasperating tales of things that happened to make certain weddings memorable. Forgotten rings, the antics of attendants, annoying photographers, collapsing cakes and, yes, a bridegroom with hiccups feature in my wedding stories. But none of those unpredictable events signalled anything about the married life that was to follow. Behind all the fun and frustration, there was always hope that each marriage held a deeper blessing in store. If a wedding is to symbolize a profound truth about our relationship with God, surely this is it: the wedding feast is only the beginning; God holds deeper blessing in store for us, no matter what goes wrong.

And things *do* go wrong in the most faithful of lives, not only at weddings. I remembered significant conversations with many guests in workshops I led at the MacLeod Centre using the work of an American theologian, W. Paul Jones. Jones' work in the book *Theological Worlds: Alternative Rhythms of Christian Belief* has offered many people a way of looking at Jesus that can help them make sense of their lives. They've come to understand why some people hold dearly to one point of view about Jesus while others relate to completely different biblical images about his life, his death and his love. Differences of faithful perspective often relate to the different life situations we've faced – and the deep questions about God stirred up by those situations. In program sessions, I often heard how people felt distanced in worship when the words proclaimed about Jesus didn't take into account the struggles they faced.

At such times, people felt they were just going through the motions required of them by local liturgy. Through Jones' analysis, we began to see how the promise God offers in Jesus can speak in different symbols, to different situations, holding out hope for deeper blessing – blessing appropriate to the needs of different hearts. We often tried to imagine how a single worship service could offer God's promise to people facing different challenges and seeking different gifts from God.

I wanted to draw on the insight from these conversations and address listeners who had faced quite different challenges or crises in the flow of their lives. I hoped to remind each and every one of us that God will respond to us in whatever situation we find personally challenging with an abundance we may not yet have tasted. I chose the symbol of the cup of salvation to link the wine at the wedding to the celebration of communion. In Iona Abbey at Sunday communion, we pass large chalices of wine around the church. Each person is welcome to receive and to hand on the cup to the next person. "The cup of salvation" is a phrase many people use when sharing the cup with their neighbour. When it came my turn to receive the cup the day I preached, my neighbour whispered those words to me. I drank with a refreshed sense of the gift I needed that day, the gift of courage to make it through a crisis that had just broken open within our staff group.

So many people, staff and guests alike, came to me during the week to thank me for this sermon. It seemed to be a timely reminder of an eternal truth – that God in Christ holds out deeper blessing for us, especially in a moment when things go wrong. On many days, our familiar daily rituals of prayer – whether in Jewish gesture, Celtic poem or morning office – will connect us to God with a regularity we can trust. But when a crisis strikes, when the wine runs out, when we are running on empty, we need to drink deeply of deeper blessing. Then the cup of salvation holds what we truly need.

The way I am

Here is a series of Scripture readings and dialogues on the theme of relationships, written for a service of Commitment during Youth Festival at the island centres. I chose to use the Jesus and Peter format developed by John Bell and Graeme Maule in their book *Jesus and Peter: Off the Record Conversations* (Wild Goose Publications, 1999) because its humour readily connects with young people. Worship can draw a laugh out of us, a laugh that opens up an awkward question we might otherwise leave unvoiced, a laugh that opens us up to a deeper truth. I hoped a humorous framework might help young people reflect on some of the complicated edges of relationships that are important to them.

Dialogue One:

Reader One: Now large crowds were travelling with Jesus; and he turned and said to them, "Whoever comes to me and does not hate father and mother, wife and children, brothers and sisters, yes and even life itself, cannot be my disciple." (Luke 14.25-26)

Reader Two: "Is there anyone among you who, if your child asks for a fish, will give a snake instead? Or if the child asks for an egg, will give a scorpion? If all of you know how to give good gifts to your children, how much more will the heavenly Father give the Holy Spirit to those who ask him!" (Luke 11.11-13)

Peter: Jesus?

Jesus: Yes, Peter?

Peter: Ummmm…

Jesus: Yes, Peter?

Peter: I don't get it, Jesus.

Jesus: What's that, Peter?

Peter: This afternoon, you said to the crowd that to follow you, they'd have to hate father and mother…and really, the whole family. Or else they can't be your disciple. Does that mean…

Jesus: Mean what, Peter?

Peter: Does that mean I'm supposed to hate my wife…and my mother-in-law? Does that mean I'm not supposed to go home again?

Jesus: No, Peter.

Peter: But Jesus, you said…

Jesus: Yes, Peter. I was trying to get people's attention. To get them to think about commitment.

Peter: Commitment? Commitment to what?

Jesus: Commitment to God. Commitment to living God's way.

Peter: But I thought the law said we were to *honour* father and mother. Not hate them. Isn't family important to you, Jesus?

Jesus: How do I pray, Peter?

Peter: On your knees, I guess.

Jesus: No, no. What did I teach you to say? How do I call on God?

Peter: Our Father in Heaven.

Jesus: Right.

Peter: So…

Jesus: So family is important, Peter. It's just not the only important thing. And maybe not the most important thing.

Peter: What is the most important thing?

Jesus: God's kingdom, Peter. God's family.

Peter: So I can go home for supper tonight? And eat with my wife and my mother-in-law?

Jesus: Yes, Peter.

Peter: But I'm not talking to my mother-in-law right now. She's nagged me once too often.

Jesus: About what, Peter?

Peter: About bringing you home for dinner. And introducing you to my sister-in-law.

Jesus: Are you inviting me for dinner tonight, Peter?

Peter: Yes, please, Jesus. So you can talk to my mother-in-law.

Jesus: So you don't have to, Peter?

Peter: Weeeeell…

Jesus: She's a good woman, Peter. Try to see her as a person, not as a label.

Peter: She thinks you're a good man, Jesus. That's why she wants you to meet her daughter.

Jesus: Don't worry, Peter. I'll talk to your mother-in-law…and your sister-in-law.

Peter: About what, Jesus?

Jesus: About the kingdom of God, I expect.

Peter: I don't think that's what they have in mind.

Jesus: That's okay, Peter. It's what I have in mind. And they'll just have to take me as I am!

Dialogue Two:

Reader One: "This is my commandment, that you love one another as I have loved you. No one has greater love than this, to lay down one's life for one's friend. You are my friends if you do what I ask you." (John 15.12-14)

Reader Two: "You have heard it said, 'You shall love your neighbour and hate your enemy.' But I say to you, 'Love your enemies and pray for those who hurt you, so that you may be children of your Father in heaven.' " (Matthew 5.42-45a)

Peter: Jesus?

Jesus: Yes, Peter?

Peter: I'm confused.

Jesus: Again, Peter?

Peter: It's about friends and enemies.

Jesus: Yes, Peter. What about friends and enemies?

Peter: I'm not sure who's who anymore.

Jesus: Does it matter, Peter? Do you need some enemies?

Peter: Not really. But I seem to have a few enemies.

Jesus: For example?

Peter: The Roman soldiers, for example. They can stop us any time. Make us carry their packs for a mile. Just like that. No thanks at all. I hate it. They have so much power.... And that short tax collector. You know the one. He cheated us. He's an enemy, too.

Jesus: Peter, do you remember what I said about soldiers?

Peter: *(sighs)* Don't carry the pack for just one mile. Carry it for two.

Jesus: Right. Turn an enemy into a friend by showing a little generosity. A little kindness.

Peter: A little craziness, if you ask me.

Jesus: It's not crazy. It's love.

Peter: It won't work.

Jesus: Have you tried it?

Peter: Uh…no. Not yet.

Jesus: Well, now's your chance. That short tax collector. His name's Zacchaeus. He's invited us for tea.

Peter: Oh, no. We're not going to eat with him and his friends.

Jesus: Yes, we are.

Peter: People will talk. They'll say we mix with the wrong kind of people.

Jesus: Peter, the "wrong kind of people" need the right kind of friends.

Peter: People like us?

Jesus: People who will take them as they are.

Dialogue Three:

Reader One: Now as they went on their way, Jesus entered a certain village where a woman named Martha welcomed him into her home. She had a sister named Mary, who sat at the Lord's feet and listened to what he was saying. (Luke 10.38-39)

Reader Two: And they gave a dinner for Jesus. Martha served and her brother Lazarus was one of those at table with him. Mary took a pound of costly perfume, anointed Jesus' feet and wiped them with her hair. And the house was filled with the fragrance of the perfume. (John 12.2-3)

Peter: Uh, Jesus?

Jesus: Yes, Peter.

Peter: Have you ever been in love?

Jesus: Why do you ask?

Peter: Well, it's Mary. They say she fancies you.

Jesus: Who says?

Peter: Uh, well… James and John.

Jesus: Did you ever think that they might fancy her?

Peter: Well, no… But you do talk to her.

Jesus: Yes, I do. Mary's a good listener.

Peter: But she's a…woman.

Jesus: Yes, she is. And she asks good questions.

Peter: But…she's a woman.

Jesus: And…

Peter: Well, men and women…are made for each other in a special way. You know, like the Bible says. It's not good to be alone.

Jesus: Am I alone, Peter?

Peter: Well, no. Almost never.

Jesus: It's true that some men and some women share a path that God sets for them together. And for others, God sets a different path. But we still need each other, whatever path we take. Friends and family, lovers and loners, we all need each other on the way. Mary gives me a good conversation. I enjoy that.

Peter: *(pause)* Jesus?

Jesus: Yes, Peter.

Peter: What do I give you?

Jesus: A good argument.

Peter: Is that all?

Jesus: It's good enough, Peter. I love you just the way you are.

A prayer:

God of love and loving,
tonight we pray for all the people who matter to us:

We pray for our friends –
old and new,
near and far,
those who are dear to us
and those who have disappointed us.
May your love strengthen our friendships
and show us how to care for one another.

We pray for the members of our families –
those who live close to us
and those who may have drifted away;
those who give us encouragement
and help us through good times and hard times;
and those whom we find hard to understand,
hard to love or get along with.

May your love strengthen our family relationships
and show us how to care for one another.

We pray for our neighbours –
those we know and trust
and those who seem strange and distant;
We pray for people we have considered enemies,
and for people around us who haven't mattered at all to us.
Help us recognize the gifts and opportunities you offer us
through the many relationships that make up our communities.
May your love strengthen our communities
and show us how to care for one another.

We pray for the beloved people in our lives –
those we cherish and those who return our love and affection,
those who attract our attention and ignite our desire,
those whose love gives us joy and hope for the future.
May we never take such people for granted,
nor cling too close and so smother the love we share.
May your love strengthen our tenderness
and show us how to care for one another.

And we pray for ourselves –
that we may recognize in ourselves
the gifts you have given to make each of us unique and valuable,
and the possibility you offer for us to make a difference for the good
in every life we touch.
Amen.

Reading between the lines

The Iona Community has a long history of bringing young people to
Iona for celebration and exploration. The MacLeod Centre, where I
worked, was built on the site of the former youth camp, which hosted
hundreds of young people each summer in very basic conditions.
"The Mac" is a much more comfortable and better-equipped building

intended to welcome young people and families in a relaxed setting to explore questions of current interest and to enjoy each other's company. At some point each summer, The Mac becomes the base for a Youth Festival, a week-long event that brings about a hundred young people to both island centres. There is a lively program of workshops and entertainment drawing together young people from a wide variety of backgrounds.

Alongside the Festival, daily services take place as usual in the Abbey, offering interested young people a chance to take leadership roles from time to time. The Wednesday evening service is on the theme of commitment. On many weeks, it is planned and led by guests, assisted by program staff. The service invites participants to reflect on some aspect of Jesus' ministry that can make a difference to the way we live. I wrote this set of three Jesus and Peter conversations after talking with young people about the theme for Wednesday's service. Relationships were front and centre in their minds and on the agenda for discussion that week.

As I thought through the kinds of relationships Jesus addressed in his teaching, I recognized how challenging his words can be at a time in our lives when relationships often make all the difference about the way we feel about ourselves. Family relationships can be difficult for young people who want some independence but have not yet had much experience making decisions with deep consequences. Choosing friends and relating to those who are not friends create all kinds of ethical dilemmas. And then there are relations of the heart, poignant at any age and crucially important. What does commitment to Jesus Christ offer young people caught up in this complex web of relationships? The Jesus and Peter format offered a way to lift up complexities with a little grin and to affirm that struggling in relationships is not unusual.

During the service, young people read the dialogues with appropriate emphasis. Between each scene, we sang the chant *Take, O take me as I am*. Its text, found in Chapter 1 in the reflection *Born Again?*, is especially meaningful to young people. When we are young, our self-esteem is vulnerable if relationships turn sour. It is good news to trust that the love God offers us through Christ is dependable, no matter what family or others say about us. Knowing ourselves as beloved to God can also strengthen us to form relationships with people on the fringe of our circles. When we have a strong sense of our own worth in God's eyes, we can risk taking a stand for those whose worth is denied by others. The dialogues raise questions about our relationships. The song proclaims the gift we need from God to commit ourselves to relationships that are healthy and life-giving.

It was also my intention to open up some important aspects of biblical interpretation in these dialogues. Young people are very perceptive about teachings that contradict each other. Many are searching for a kind of coherent ethical code to help them sort through ambiguity and recognize hypocrisy. But the New Testament is full of teachings that contradict each other. Jesus taught in parables and paradox – things not easy to codify. The teachings on family in the New Testament are a key example. Jesus makes provocative comments, calling disciples to turn away from family whereas authors of various letters often insert rather stiff statements of how members of a household should relate to each other. This topic could fill a college course. Still, that night I hoped to lift up what I believe to be the heart of Jesus' message – that all relationships are both judged and blessed from the perspective of the kingdom of God. No relationship is more important than the relationship God offers us through Jesus Christ. This will transform all other relationships because it transforms the way we know and value ourselves. This key relationship will sort and heal and guide all other relationships, a truth for us at any time of our lives but especially important when we're young and relationships so key to our identity.

A parable for Advent

Jesus had such a knack for telling stories and drawing examples from things we encounter every day. I often imagine that stories recorded *about* Jesus were first told by someone on the scene, fascinated by what they'd heard *from* him. Eventually those stories caught the ears of one of the evangelists, who retold them with a bit of their own spin to help us get the point. Here, I feel a bit like my imagined evangelists. I am telling a story based on something that really happened – not to me, but to some good friends. I have woven it together as the storyteller, drawing its threads together as faithfully as I could, hoping to honour the faithfulness at its heart. It was Advent when the wonder in the story emerged, the same kind of wonder that we find in the stories of Jesus.

She has waited a long, long life –
nearly 90 years.
She never knew her mother,
who died in the labour of love
called birth.
She has never even seen her mother's picture,
her mother's smile.
Nearly 90,
she longs to know what her mother looks like
– so she'll recognize her mother when they meet in heaven.
She never knew her father, either,
swallowed in the aftermath of the Great War.
His family raised her
as an only child of a generation,
tended by maiden aunts,
lost to her mother's family
for nearly 90 years.
She grew into a wise and loving woman,
herself a cherished mother.
Still, the quiet longing to see her own mother's face lingered
as she emerged the last of a generation,
orphaned,

widowed,
her children the only proof of family.
Or so it seemed.

Children, being children,
take matters into their own hands.
There *had* been a brother.
What of him?
His children?
His grandchildren?
Records searched.
Loose ends traced.
At last a name.
At last an address.
A letter sent.
No answer.
Weeks pass.
Another letter.
No answer.
Months pass.
The trail grows cold.
She smiles wisely.
After nearly 90 years,
who can blame them
if they do not want to know
me?

But then the phone rings.
A new voice.
A familiar name.
Telling of fairy-tale complications.
Someone moves house.
Mail collects unsorted
for months.
Then the mail is claimed.

One letter, two letters found.
And the new voice is calling
the very next day.
He is her first cousin.
He had been told of her birth.
But her trail had grown cold.
Still he wondered about her.
Who she was.
And now he wants to know her,
who she is,
after nearly 90 years.
Are there pictures? she wonders.
Many pictures! he promises.
My mother; your aunt,
Is she there?
Let us look and see
together.

Here is a story,
a true story still unfolding.
Here is a real family
still searching its truth.
Here is hope,
ancient hope still alive and growing.
Hope,
the labour of love for nearly 90 years.
It is born again
For her.
In her.
It is born again
For us.
In us.
When we trust the promise of the angels.
With God, nothing is impossible.

Hope wears a fresh face,
sparkles in eyes new and old
after nearly 90 years.
And more.
Hope labours
for us;
in us;
to bring love to birth
when we think our trail has grown cold.
Let us trust the promise of angels.
For God with us
nothing is impossible.

God of Life,
in our hopeless times,
in our barren moments,
come to us and be with us.
Hold out hope for us that new life can stir again within us.
God of Mystery,
confounding our expectations,
meeting us when we least expect to find you,
stay with us on our journey.
Walk beside us
day by day,
year after year.
Lead us to heaven.
Lead us home
where at last we will meet you
face to face.
Amen.

Reading between the lines

The parable simplifies a very moving episode in the life of friends. I
heard it told, bit by bit, over several months. Possibility. Excitement.

Challenge. Silence. Discouragement. It was approaching Advent when the surprising phone call came, offering new possibility to the very faithful woman at the story's heart. There was a powerful sense of a wish coming true, of lifelong prayers answered. Yet things happened in an unexpected way, beyond plan or coincidence. As George MacLeod is often quoted as saying, "If you believe in co-incidence, you'll lead a dull life."

As I listened to my friend marvel at the possibility of seeing her mother's face, I thought of the lives of Elizabeth and Zechariah turned upside down by the arrival of a baby after so many years of longing. Their situation was the reverse of my friend's, the longing of a lonely child to discover a yearned-for parent before it was too late. Still, she had held out hope at least as long as Zechariah and Elizabeth, and had never surrendered her quiet dignity, whatever happened.

I told this story in an Advent worship service in order to play with the role reversal: child longing for parent, offering a different miracle of hope, one not rooted in the conception of a baby. The emphasis on the wondrous births of Advent and Christmas can sometimes be hard to claim for those who do not have children, and perhaps never will. Yet the faithful yearning of this grandmother speaks to many of us and the ways in which we do carry on fruitful lives even when a wish or a prayer has not found fulfillment. I deliberately chose a spare style with short, simple sentences, partly to avoid details that would give away my friend's identity, and partly to create a feeling of a life lived with some crucial details missing. The style also echoes the character of this woman who would not want too much made of her life. But for many of my listeners I know that she is a parable of hope and faithfulness. A quiet reminder that it is never too late for God to surprise us with delight.

And yes, there was a picture.
She has seen her mother's face after nearly 90 years.

Is it enough?

Each week on Tuesday evening, a service of Prayers for Healing is held on Iona. It is part of the ministry of the Iona Community's Prayer Circle, which maintains a global network of people who pray for others. This ministry has a long and deep history within the Community that runs alongside its work for justice and peace. Prayer is the foundation of both commitments, seeking God's healing grace for the well-being of individuals and for the world as a whole. The service has a very simple structure that includes a Bible reading and often a brief meditation on that reading. Very often one of the stories about Jesus' healing touch is read. However, during Holy Week one year, we chose for the evening services Scripture readings to follow Mark's account of the days between Jesus' entry into Jerusalem and his Crucifixion. The story of the widow in Mark 12.41-44 was chosen for the Tuesday evening service.

The widow's voice:
Is it enough,
the penny of my prayers?
Offering to you
my wrinkled worries,
the ache of my anxiety,
hardly seems like gratitude, O God.

Is it enough,
the penny of my prayers?
A widowed heart
has lost its innocence.
Gnarled with grief,
my years spill their tears
before you, O God.
Is it enough to bring
a soul laden with loss?
doubt-drenched whispers
seeking your embrace?

Can it be enough
to add another penny
from hearts hurting for the world?
We spend more tears
for those in terror
or trouble of their own making
and the making,
the shaking,
the taking of others.
Our trembling hands
drop our coins of concern,
word by word,
thought by thought,
one sigh at a time,
into your healing hands, O God.
Can this be enough?

(silence)

Jesus' voice:
Truly,
I tell you,
out of your poverty
you have given all you have.
In the hands of God,
in the heart of God,
it *is* enough.

Reading between the lines

Each week, before the service of prayers for healing, guests at the centres join in conversation about the Iona Community's ministry of healing. The Community has learned over the years that it is helpful for guests to talk about their ideas and experience connected to healing before the service. The service is powerful in its simplicity.

Conversations help us prepare ourselves and support each other, especially when someone feels a current situation very deeply. Often in these conversations, I heard people talk about prayer in their lives, whether or not prayer contributes to healing. Stories lifted up a range of experience. Sometimes prayer for healing had led someone to a powerful encounter with God. Yet just as often, someone would recount disappointment, doubt, even anger when heartfelt prayer seemed to have made no difference. No change, no healing was apparent. Why pray, then? Why pray for people who are just names on a list? Why pray for intractable situations of suffering in the world? Why pray when too often God does not seem to respond?

These questions express the deep anguish of doubt. There is no simple answer because such questions grow out of life stories, and stories are never satisfied with an answer. Stories call for a listening ear and a companion as the story continues to unfold. The same questions were first put to me when I was a very young minister, at a time when I had studied more than I had lived. Such questions often came from faithful people who were deeply puzzled by the tragedies life had dealt them. They worried and wondered deeply if they had let God down somehow because they themselves felt let down. I only began to reframe my sense of God's presence in the midst of tragedy when I talked to the widows of my parish. Widows taught me the power of prayer to claim God as companion through the depths of despair – and beyond.

To honour these faithful widows, I wanted to work with the story of another faithful widow as our companion in the prayers during Holy Week. By the end of Holy Week, God will have surrendered earthly power to defeat the power of death through self-giving love. How can one life sacrificed be enough? This widow gave all she had out of love. It was only a tiny gift. How could it be enough? Often, when we are faced with the stark reality of power that stands against us as illness, as injustice, as isolation, prayer is all we have to give. In prayer, we surrender to God an outcry, a plea. We remember our hopes before God and confess our helplessness, our fear, our anger, our sorrow. In the depths of our need, this is all we have to give. Is this enough? How can this be enough?

In a few poetic lines, I tried to offer these feelings and fears to God, using the images from Mark's story. I believe that prayer, at its heart, is surrendering ourselves into the presence of God. Prayer is self-giving, nothing more and nothing less. When all we have to offer is fear or anger or sorrow, when this is all we are, it is enough that we give this over to God. God will bear our gifts, bear us through the darkness and pain known to all widowed hearts. Christ died to show us this. And to promise us that love will dawn on us again. The widows have shown me this truth: It is enough.

3

Gather Us In!

At the heart of Columba's community on Iona lay a ministry of hospitality to pilgrims and passers-by. Scottish people share this hospitable nature, as I found in my three years there. The Iona Community's island centres draw on this double heritage. Once space for housing guests had been constructed by George MacLeod's teams of builders, the Community's vision of drawing people into community through shared work and worship took on new shapes. There are fascinating stories of this sharing as it developed over the years. The kind of accommodation and programming provided, the times and style of worship and the nature of shared work have all changed during that time. Of course, I know only a few of those years in detail, but my work there flourished because of the Community's long-cherished commitment to hospitality. Much wisdom has been gained through the experience of forming and re-forming community in the island centres, week after week. Yet each week is unique, and experience teaches us to expect the unexpected!

Offering hospitality is not the same as meeting expectations, I learned. For example, those who come to Iona expecting to find a quiet (and therefore "spiritual") place may not have reckoned that more than a hundred thousand visitors come to the island, mainly from the middle of March until the end of October. During this visitor season, nearly one hundred guests will be welcomed to the Abbey and the MacLeod

Centre each week. Voluntary staff come and go amid regular traffic that sustains the life of a working island. Local islanders share in many forms of hospitality, too, welcoming visitors to their bed-and-breakfast accommodation, to their shops, hotels, restaurants and tours by land or sea. Iona is a busy place for much of the year. Those who work to provide hospitality can often only snatch conversations with each other on the roadside when responsibilities pull us in different directions.

Amid all this coming and going, the Iona Community island centres do not aim to provide quiet retreats. Instead, guests are invited to discover what they have to share with each other and to recognize God in our midst in unanticipated encounters. Relationships are the seed bed of spirituality – for when we open ourselves to meet each other, God can move in that space we have created in our lives. Our spiritual discoveries in community can be every bit as renewing as time spent in solitary contemplation – and, for many people, life-changing. Yet to move out of our preferred private patterns into an ever-changing experience of one another, we need a spirit of adventure some days. When we grow weary, we need the resilience God's grace alone can supply. Staff and guest alike have much to discover about ourselves when we can risk ourselves in relationships, even for a little while.

The selections in this chapter lift up a variety of challenges I faced during my three years tending to details of hospitality on Iona. Managing a guest centre raises myriad details each week, mundane and yet essential, just to be sure everyone has a bed and every meal is served (approximately!) on time. Details are also important when newcomers are welcomed to worship. In the Abbey, some guests are puzzled by the repetition of page numbers and book titles and invitations to stand or sit, which staff dutifully rehearse service after service. Yet these details are offered for the sake of those present who have never attended worship before, or who do not speak English well or read quickly. All these people come to worship in the Abbey *every week*. The Community's staff try to welcome them in the midst of those who are much more familiar with church customs. Wherever I attend worship now, I am newly sensitive to the details offered to include a stranger and to those local customs taken for granted and never explained.

The first reflection in this chapter is a celebration of detail offered especially for my Iona colleagues who occasionally grow weary in well-doing. The second piece is fed partly by my encounters with people who do not feel welcome in their own skin. It focuses on gospel hospitality offered in Jesus' very human life. The third, an excerpt from a service designed to include children, proved surprisingly controversial. Children, it seems, often find no greater welcome among those who flock to the Abbey than they did among those flocking to hear Jesus. The words of Jesus recorded in Matthew's Gospel are pertinent whenever and wherever we come to worship: "Whoever welcomes one such child in my name welcomes me." Imagine a child worshipping alongside you as you enter this section. What might draw him or her into the company of Jesus?

Entertaining angels

This service was developed for the opening week of the season when our first set of guests joined staff for the spring cleaning of the centres. New members of the resident staff were settling in, and now faced the imminent and inescapable prospect of centres filled with guests. New volunteers had just taken up their posts and were learning to work with each other. The responsibilities that lay ahead were all too real at that moment. To help us reflect on the significance of offering hospitality, I chose two biblical texts, Genesis 18.1-8 and Luke 10.38-42, to be read as part of a dialogue with several voices. As well, Hebrews 13.2 is chanted between sections of the dialogue. We gathered around a table set down the centre of the Abbey, laid with symbols of the many kinds of work we would undertake together.

A dialogue with Scripture

Abraham looked up and saw three men standing near him. When he saw them, he ran from the tent entrance to meet them, and bowed down to the ground.

Abraham: My lord, if I find favour with you, do not pass by your servant. Let a little water be brought, and wash your feet. Rest yourselves under the tree. Let me bring a little bread that you may refresh yourselves, and after that you may pass on – since you have come to your servant.

So they said, "Do as you have said." And Abraham hastened into the tent to Sarah.

Abraham: Make ready quickly three measures of choice flour, knead it, and make cakes.

Abraham ran to the herd, and took a calf, tender and good, and gave it to the servant, who hastened to prepare it. Then he took curds and milk and the calf that he had prepared, and set it before them; and he stood by them under the tree while they ate.

> *Do not neglect to show hospitality to strangers,*
> *for by doing that some have entertained angels*
> *without knowing it.*

Now as they went on their way, Jesus entered a certain village, where a woman named Martha welcomed him into her home. She had a sister named Mary, who sat at the Lord's feet and listened to what he was saying. But Martha was distracted by her many tasks; so she came to him and asked,

Martha: Lord, do you not care that my sister has left me to do all the work by myself? Tell her then to help me.

But the Lord answered her:

Jesus: Martha, Martha, you are worried and distracted by many things; there is need of only one thing. Mary has chosen the good part, which will not be taken away from her.

> *Do not neglect to show hospitality to strangers,*
> *for by doing that some have entertained angels*
> *without knowing it.*

Sarah: Abraham! How could you bring three strangers home without some warning?

Abraham: We can't let guests pass this way without inviting them in. It's our duty.

Sarah: But the tent floor hadn't been swept. The duvet covers were still on the line. And the dusting not done! Duty takes time, Abraham.

Abraham: All they needed was a little bit of bread.... And I know how wonderful your bread is, my dear. Fit for friend or stranger.

Sarah: A little bit of bread, you say? Three measures of choice flour. That's a hundred cakes you ordered, my *dear*. A lit-tle bit of bread. The feast took a day to prepare. And you! You stood under that tree and watched.

Jesus: Sarah, Sarah, you are worried and distracted by many things; there is need of only one thing.

> *Do not neglect to show hospitality to strangers,*
> *for by doing that some have entertained angels*
> *without knowing it.*

Martha: Mary, get up off that chair and help me chop these vegetables.

(*Pause*)

Mary, put down that newspaper and grate this cheese.

(*Pause*)

Mary, if I have to chop these vegetables and grate this cheese, the least you could do is sweep the common-room floor.

(*Pause*)

Mary, Jesus is coming down the path. Did you put fresh oil in the lamp? Are there flowers on the table?

(*Pause*)

Welcome, Jesus. You'll have to excuse the mess. Mary, at least give the man your chair. You could help me serve the tea.

Jesus: Martha, Martha, you are worried and distracted by many things; there is need of only one thing.

*Do not neglect to show hospitality to strangers,
for by doing that some have entertained angels
without knowing it.*

A reflection for our own situation

There is need of only one thing.
And what would that one thing be, Jesus?

Here we are.
Nearly 50 volunteers and residents.
A hundred or so islanders.
Our first set of guests for the season has arrived.
More will come.
In fact, more than 2500 guests will visit our island centres,
and 100,000 will come to the island over the next few months.
Together, neighbour and stranger,
we will welcome each other into a small part of our lives.

On Iona we share in an amazing ministry of hospitality.
A ministry of astonishing variety in which we will indeed encounter
   angels
within the tide of strangers and visitors who wash up on these
   shores.
I daresay that during our stay, short or long,
someone will astonish each of us
and teach us something of God's surprising ways.
But could it ever be that in this place of astonishing hospitality,
any of us will find ourselves worried and distracted by many things?

Too many angels with too much luggage who arrive late for dinner?
Yet another touring angel who asks us where to find Macbeth's tomb
– just when we wanted to head out for a quiet walk on our own?
A not-so-angelic angel who wakes us up late one night
– the night before we have to make an early ferry?

This is a place filled with a host of distractions,
details that are important to this ministry of hospitality;
details that can be worrisome when they don't all fall into place:
details that can make us anxious
when we find ourselves in the swirl of hard work with less time or
    energy than we wish.
And Jesus tells us there is need of only one thing.
Just what would that one thing be?

Dear friends and neighbours,
dear guests and fellow pilgrims,
Mary has a word to speak
to all of us for whom a welcome in a strange place is a sign of God's
    love.
In the midst of all these details
there is need of only one thing.
Mary gave herself.
And her gift was enough.

Abraham and Sarah gave themselves.
Yes, there was an amazing feast and all that bread.
But that old couple had volunteered themselves on a pilgrimage with
    God.
And they became parents to God's gift of new life.

Yes, Martha, the details are important.
Details show that we care for others.
But the details mean nothing
if they cannot be offered with a cheerful heart and a listening ear.
For the heart, the ear, the eyes, the smile
convey the gift of welcome.
One thing is enough.
That we give ourselves.

In the midst of all the distracting details
and any anxiety or frustration they stir up within us,
let us remember that we are enough.
We are enough for God.
Jesus Christ gave himself to promise us this.
We are enough for God.
And the angels will find what they need
with us –
and within us.
For this is how God chooses to be found.

(A table had been laid down the centre aisle of the Abbey Church, bearing items from each area of work that staff undertake on behalf of the Iona Community. The prayer was used to open the season of our work together.)

God, our Maker
for nourishing gifts that strengthen us day by day
for cooks and creativity
for vegetables and vitality
for porridge and for pudding
for housekeepers and hospitality
for clean towels and clean hands
for warm fires and warm hearts
we thank you, God.
Through all these things, bless us, O God.
GOD, WE BLESS YOU.

For organizing talents that let days and weeks run smoothly
for phones and friendly voices
for information and lists, and rotas, and more lists
for money used for your purposes
and for those who keep track of it
for fairly traded goods and fair exchange
for books to inspire and music to cheer us
we thank you, God.

Through all these things, bless us, O God.
GOD, WE BLESS YOU.

For the wonder of conversation
and the wonder of candle flame
for flip charts and flippant good cheer
for songs to sing and music to tap toes
for art and beauty and space to imagine
for chairs in their places and light bulbs that work
for mending and building, with hands and within hearts
for luggage lifted and spirits lifted
for all the bells that ring and all the prayers said
we give you thanks, O God.
Through all these things, bless us, O God.
GOD, WE BLESS YOU.

To you, O God,
we bring who we are,
gifts and fears,
hopes and memories,
ordinary things of the life we share.
We bring our skill and experience,
our energy and laughter,
our patience and goodwill,
ordinary things the world needs.
We bring what we have,
tools of our hands and hearts
ordinary things of the earth.
We ask you to bless our tools,
our time
and our talents,
in all the ways you can use us.
So make astonishing things possible through us
in this, your holy place.
Amen.

Reading between the lines

Iona Abbey is filled with remnants of beautiful Celtic interlace and bits of knot work carved on its pillars and around the baptismal font. Interlace looks like braided lines – though when you trace a finger along the braiding, you may find the strands merging into a single line. I like to braid parts of Scripture, using different voices, allowing the overlapping of stories to lead us to a common truth. I do not mean to diminish the delicious detail in the texts I weave together. Rather, I hope that by putting familiar details from one story alongside familiar details from another, we may recognize something new as one storyline leads into another.

At the opening of our guest season each year, there were many details to attend to all at once in both centres. So many things to learn. So many things that could go wrong, given a chance! All in the name of hospitality. It was easy for staff members, old and new, to lose patience or heart under pressure. The story about Martha and Mary is read often on Iona as we reflect on the ministry of hospitality. It is a story that makes some people angry – angry at Mary for not doing her share; angry at Jesus for expecting special attention. Such people take Martha's side. The story will provoke us when we feel this way. Mary has chosen the "good" part, says Jesus. He is not comparing Mary to Martha. He is affirming one thing about Mary's choice. I wanted to affirm that choice as I see it, while giving voice to what can be a major frustration in the ministry of hospitality: too many details and too little time.

The story of Abraham and his visitors is equally famous in Christian tradition, though perhaps not so familiar to my listeners. I often wondered why Sarah played such a passive role when Abraham placed on her the responsibilities of nomadic hospitality. I could easily play Martha's role on Sarah's behalf, so that's the tone in which I wrote Sarah's part. The identity of the visitors is elusive, but tradition has it they were angels, sent by God to begin the adventures of God's people through the birth of Isaac, son of Sarah and Abraham's old age.

Their mysterious visit echoes in the verse from the Book of Hebrews, repeating its invitation to look for angels among those whom we are called to serve. I had already worked on Iona long enough to know it is not always easy to find an angelic side in every guest or stranger!

My own sense of the Gospel comes to the fore in the affirmation that we are enough for God. At the Abbey we often struggled with the desire for things to be perfect – and yet they never were. Whenever things go wrong, it is easy to feel culpable or inadequate deep inside. We often take out our feelings of inadequacy on those around us through our anxious tempers and edgy demands. It was no different on Iona than in the churches where I've served. One thing about the work of the island centres is amazing, though. Week by week, guests leave feeling welcomed and cared for even during times when staff members are under stress. Through the consistent appreciation offered by guests, I learned to let go of my own worries about making the MacLeod Centre a perfect space and place. It was more important to do what Mary did: to attend to each guest with attention, face to face. I tried to inspire and support my staff team to trust what we offered together. For we are enough. God knows this better than we do. And so, we discovered, do our guests. This is amazing grace!

Bread and stories

At the island centres, the pulse of conversation would always beat faster when we sat down to lunch. Lunch is simple: a nourishing vegetable soup and delicious homemade bread. The bread from the Abbey is famous. You can buy a tea towel with the recipe printed on it! Conversation, like the bread, is fresh each day, for the morning's program provides food for thought. When I prepared this service, our theme for the week was words. Big words. Not words with lots of syllables but words painted in large proportion, sailing from the rafters in the MacLeod Centre. As I listened to people marvel at each other's creativity over lunch, I had an idea for a service in which spoken words might also float before us, colliding and calling to us. To reflect on words, there seemed no better Scripture than John 1.1-4, 10-14. The words it connects to the Word of God became the fabric for my spoken collage.

The readers' chorus was done by four different voices, reading the words and phrases in fairly rapid succession but slowing toward the end of each section. The chant "Jesus Christ, Jesus Christ" was sung as a prayer to call us beyond words. The music provided is taken from the collection *There Is One Among Us*, edited by John Bell, © 1999 Wild Goose Resource Group.

Voice One:

In the beginning was the Word. And the Word was with God. And the Word was God.

Voice Two:

In the Word was life,
And the life was the light of all people.

Readers' Chorus:

Word
Sound
Language
Letters
Sign
Speech
Conversation

The Word became flesh
The Word is very near to you, it is in your mouth and in your heart.
My word shall not return to me empty
The Word is very near to you
Word
Sound
Language
Speech
Conversation
Word
My word!
The Word
The Word became flesh and dwelt among us.

Voice Three:
The Word became flesh and dwelt among us.
These words from the Gospel of John name Jesus as the Word of
    God:
God's Word born, crying and wriggling with human life.
God's Word – in the flesh,
God's conversation with the world,
walking beside us,
sitting at table with us,
pitching a tent in our midst
and living with us.
That's how the Greek text reads:
God's Word "pitched its tent" on our campsite
and a story that has touched us all one way or another began its
    telling.
God's Word isn't a neat definition of the meaning of life.
It's not a clear command of what we must do.
God's Word is a life.
A story.
A conversation that took flesh in Jesus,

the man of stories and conversations.
God's Word takes flesh in our lives,
people of stories and conversation.
God's Word is very near us.
In our mouths.
In our hearts.
Can you taste it?
Can you feel it?
Can you live it?

Refrain

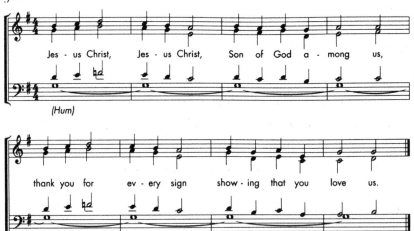

Readers' Chorus:
The Word became flesh.
Flesh.
Bodies.
My body.
Your body.
The Body of Christ.
Flesh.
Skin and muscle.
Appetite and desire.
Sweat and wrinkles.
Sagging or skin-tight.

Flesh.
Different shapes and sizes;
Different colours and textures;
Flesh.
Weigh it or exercise it.
Hate it or love it.
Flesh.

Voice Three:
The Word became flesh and dwelt among us,
full of grace and truth.
It's an uncomfortable truth –
that God's Word became flesh.
People have struggled for centuries to make Jesus more than flesh
or less than flesh.
We've made him able to read minds at a glance
and go without sleep or any other bodily need;
never subject to desire or weakness.
Still the Gospel writers record that Jesus and his friends
were found at table in many places;
They were known for enjoying a good time with unusual people.
People of the flesh.
And here we are,
people of the flesh,
lots of us not sure about our own flesh,
how to cover it or care for it,
how much to enjoy it or reduce it or reveal it.
But the Word became flesh
and so the Word knows the comforts and discomforts of the flesh –
knows our comforts and discomforts.
And that Word is full of grace and truth:
grace that accepts the flesh we are
and forgives what we might despise or want to change;
truth that reveals what is healing and life-giving

in the face of whatever it is that we crave or resist.
Grace and truth.
In the flesh.
Meant for us.
All of us.

Refrain

Flesh.
Our flesh,
blessed by the Word.
And though Scripture reminds us that creatures of flesh do not live
    by bread alone
but by every word that comes from the mouth of God,
still God's Word became bread –
daily bread,
the Bread of Life –
to be broken and shared that all may have life
    and have it abundantly –
in the flesh.

Readers' Chorus:
Bread.
Aroma.
Taste.
Texture.
Thick slices,
crusty,
heavy with grain and seed;
thin slices,
white,
refined,
host to toast,
sandwiched for Iona pilgrims.
Rye bread.

Soda bread.
Sourdough.
Unleavened bread.
Rice cake.
Oat cake.
Daily bread.
The stuff of life
in as many shapes and sizes
as the flesh of the people who eat it.
I am the bread of life.
Whoever comes to me will never be hungry.
Whoever believes in me will never thirst.

Voice Three:
Bread and stories.
That's who Jesus is:
bread, the stuff of life
and stories that make life worth living.
Bread and stories.
That's who we are:
lives caught up in stuff −
stuff that matters,
stuff we'd like to get rid of −
and stories −
stories that matter,
even the stories we'd like to be shed of −
stories that matter to God, the Word made flesh.
Bread and stories.
This is who we are;
and this is what we have to share with each other
and with Jesus
who has shared himself with us
that we might taste the grace and truth that will make us whole.

Refrain

Reading between the lines

The island centres of the Iona Community have a particular understanding of their purpose. Staff members have to interpret this purpose week by week. We say, "This is not a conference centre. Nor is it a retreat centre." We invite guests and the ever-changing group of staff to encounter each other in work and worship, through mealtime conversation, thematic discussions and recreation. Both the Abbey and the MacLeod Centre offer some programs, but never does a program involve a full day of talking about an issue. This is occasionally a disappointment to guests who seek out our centres with their experience of conferences in mind. What we do share in a week is often surprising and fresh, drawing out insight and confidence to renew us.

This meditation on Word and Bread was developed during a week at the MacLeod Centre led by Manchester artist Steve Raw. Steve has a unique ability to help people explore the words around us, inspiring them to create stunning visual expressions. People who don't fancy themselves as artistic suddenly see their letters spring to life, proclaiming gospel in powerful ways. It was a week of creative energy that burst into the centre, as huge banners of colourful words were hoisted to the ceiling to provoke our conversations.

When I planned this meditation for Thursday evening communion, I was inspired by the visual feast unfolding at the Mac. The image of a mobile was in my mind. Steve was planning to hang a colourful tapestry of letters, painted by our guests, in the centre of the church. It would silently rehearse a verse from one of the communion songs. I wanted to hang spoken symbols on invisible threads, to catch our attention in worship and help us reflect on the week just past. From John's Gospel, I picked out three key words: Word. Flesh. Bread. Here were symbols of what we had shared that week and would share that night, gathering up for us God's promise embodied in Jesus.

The word studies for this meditation grew from research I had done years before. When I was doing my doctoral studies in the 1980s, I came across interesting debate on the word we translate as "Word" in John's Gospel. The Greek, *logos*, might be better translated as "speech" or "conversation" or "dialogue." This "Word" hints at storytelling more than a combination of letters. When I discovered this, the first chapter of John came alive. Jesus wasn't simply a word that could be neatly defined and memorized, some kind of a divine slogan. No, the Word of God is alive in speech, in the give and take of conversation, listening, arguing passionately, telling a story, laughing, nodding when one of our tender memories is shared. That Word becomes flesh in Jesus, the man of stories, but it is also made flesh in his community as we share stories with each other. Sharing stories is so much a part of life on Iona week by week. I often marvelled at the trust that grew around the meal table when people opened up their lives to each other.

"Flesh" is a trickier word in the history of Christian community. "Flesh" is sometimes set against "spirit" and used to symbolize the power of sin to be overcome in human life. This view of flesh has its roots in Greek philosophy, which fed much ancient Christian teaching. It has encouraged Christians to ignore or despise our bodies and to value spiritual things as if they are somehow separate from the tangible, sweaty, pulsing lives we lead. But John insists that the Word became flesh. And that this fleshy Word was full of grace and truth. I wanted to affirm human flesh as part of God's good creation because I am aware how often people struggle with their own flesh. I sometimes saw young women at our centres eat so little at mealtime that I wondered how they kept going. They were concerned about their weight and their visual appeal. Flesh is a fashion statement. Other people struggle to accept their flesh in the face of such fashion statements, flesh that is ageing or aching or sagging. Still others have a discipline of physical exercise I admire, while some cannot move their bodies without assistance. We are people of the flesh, whether we like it or not: the same flesh that brought us face to face with God in Jesus.

And bread. The bread from our kitchens on Iona is famous. It is a wonderful part of lunchtime meals, baked fresh each morning. But bread is a complicated part of our culture, too. Young appetites often prefer the pale, purchased, mechanically sliced version that we toast in the morning. Some people need a wheat-free substitute. Others worry that too much bread will lead to too much flesh! When we name Jesus the Bread of Life, our symbol is full of complex meaning. All three words for this service are full of meanings that bump up against each other, insisting that we share our experience with each other because no single meaning, no personal significance can speak for everyone.

The readers' choruses were designed to dangle different layers of meaning before us, just as the artists in residence at the MacLeod Centre had dangled their provocative words around us all week. These sections were read at a fairly fast pace, allowing the sounds and images to collide with each other, as objects hanging on a mobile might. The words I offered, as Voice Three, were crafted in very short sentences but given at a slower, more reflective pace. The chant was slow and gentle, followed by several seconds of silence – as if the mobile had come to rest. Then, as the next section began, it was as if the wind of the Spirit breathed into our midst and set the mobile moving again, to show us something new. I am not sure how well my oral mobile worked for listeners, but I retain a powerful visual memory of the mobile in the crossing of the Abbey church (the open heart of the church where the "arms" of the building reach out to suggest the shape of a cross), gently turning to reveal its proclamation as we broke open word and bread that night. The subtle connections between the visual and the spoken word enriched both so that the Word dwelt among us again, offering grace and truth in the unexpected collision of lives gathered around the table.

Doing your best

Welcoming young children to worship is a challenge wherever your church community is located. At Iona Abbey, there are particular challenges, beginning with the amount of printed material provided for most services. The shape of the Abbey makes it hard for people sitting in one part to see other parts of the church, a particular hardship for children who want to watch what's going on. One year, I was part of a leadership team at the MacLeod Centre exploring approaches to all-age worship. We received permission to create a unique liturgy for Sunday morning, using the best of our strategies for welcoming children into worship. Knowing that children enter into anything in a more physical way than most adults, we chose texts that invite us to offer our whole selves to God: Deuteronomy 6.4-5 and Luke 10.25-28. I wrote a story for this occasion, portraying the themes of the Scripture in episodes a child could recognize. It was told in dramatic form, with three different voices portraying the various characters. Young children were invited to sit on mats laid on the floor around the storytellers. Another person gave the reflections and led the chant between sections of the story. After the reading from the Gospel of Luke, we taught the words to the chant. (The chant we used was the South African song "Reamo Leboga," whose chorus means "Together we thank you, God of ours." See p. 124 for the music and lyrics.) Then the story began:

"Guess what, Mum?" Fergie the Frog was very excited when he came home from a Frog Scout meeting.

"Did you learn to tie a knot in your tongue?" she asked.

Fergie flicked his tongue to show her it still worked. "No, no. There's going to be a competition. Scout Master Leatherlips says it's to find the best all-round frog. Umm… What's an all-round frog, Mum?"

She chuckled. "That's you after you fill up on gnat burgers and French flies."

"Are we having gnat burgers tonight?" asked Fergie hopefully.

"I'm teasing," said Mother Frog. "An all-round frog is pretty good at doing most things a frog has to do. Hopping, swimming, fly-catching…."

"I hope an all-round frog doesn't have to do math," said Fergie with a frown. "I'm not very good at math."

The first part of the competition was called "A Good Deed a Day." For one whole month, all the frog scouts had to do at least one good deed, one kind thing every day. The three frogs who did the most kind things in a month would move on to the finals.

Fergie tried very hard to be very helpful. He helped his father catch caterpillars for supper. He set the table for his mother every night. He even helped his big brother Freddie clean out his mudhole.

Freddie asked, "Are you feeling all right, Fergie? You're being too nice for a little brother."

Fergie flicked him in the head with his tongue. "I'm just being nice to win the competition."

At the end of the month, Fergie was a winner. So was his best friend, Roger. But the top frog was Webster, a frog who worked hard at school.

"I knew Webster would win," Fergie complained. "He has more brothers and sisters. More frogs to help."

"Don't complain," said his father. "You did your best. Let's see what comes next."

Reflection:
God asks us to love our neighbours.
Loving our neighbours means doing kind things for them
like looking for ways to help them,
caring about things that go wrong,
or being a friend to someone who's lonely.
Doing a good deed a day is part of loving our neighbours.
And that's part of loving God
heart, mind, soul and strength.

Chant: Chorus (Reamo leboga modimo warona) and verse 1.

Part Two:

The three little frogs had three more contests in the competition. First
came a race on land and in the water, the two places where frogs
live.

Fergie pouted, "Roger will win. He can swim faster than I can."

"Just try your best," said his mother. "You're a good hopper."

For the race the frog scouts had to hop down the path, hop through
the mud at the edge of the pond, then swim across the pond and
hop up a hill to the finish line. When Scout Master Leatherlips blew
his starting whistle, Fergie took a good leap, hopping downhill. But
the mud slowed him down. And in the pond, Roger swam right
past him. Fergie nearly caught up to Roger on the hill, but Roger
crossed the finish line a nose ahead of Fergie. Webster came third,
puffing hard as he finished.

"I came second this time," complained Fergie with a big sigh. "I'll
never win."

"Did you try your best?" asked his father.

Fergie nodded.

"That's what counts," said his mother. "Winning isn't everything, you
know."

"But winning feels better," Fergie said.

Reflection:

When we try our best to do something,
we often try hard and get tired.
Did you ever think about trying hard, trying your best
to do something for God?
When God asks us to do important things in the world –
I think God is always glad
when God knows we tried our best
with heart, mind, strength and soul –
even if it doesn't work out quite the way we planned.

Chant: *Chorus and verses 2 and 3.*

Part Three:

The next contest was for arts and crafts. The frogs could make whatever
they liked. Paint or draw or write a story. Make something…or sing
a song.

"Whatever comes from your soul," said Scout Master Leatherlips.

"Where's my soul?" Fergie asked his Mum.

Mother Frog thought for a minute. "Your soul is what makes you
special. It is what makes you different from every other frog in the
world. It's where your dreams live. And where tears and laughter
come from."

Fergie tried making different things that week. He made a mud sculpture
of a dragonfly but then he jumped on it when Freddie asked him
what it was.

"If you can't tell what it is, I won't win."

Fergie didn't feel good about any of the things he made. The night of
the judging he left the house with a piece of paper in his pocket.
No one knew what he'd done.

Roger was called on first. He proudly showed his mud sculpture.

"What is it?" asked Mr. Leatherlips.

"It's a lily pad," said Roger.

"Oh…I see…," said the Scout Master.

"I think it looks like a pancake," Freddie whispered to Fergie.

Webster had learned a song. But he was very nervous and he forgot a
few of the words. And then a few of the notes.

"Good try," said Mr. Leatherlips.

When it was Fergie's turn, he pulled out his piece of paper. "I wrote a
poem for my Mum…ahem…

Every frog has a mother
But my mum is like no other
She cooks like a dream
By the side of the stream
She laughs from her soul

With her little tadpole
And I won't trade her in on another."

When Fergie finished, every mother frog in the room was sniffling. The frogs croaked and croaked until Scout Master Leatherlips cleared his throat.

"I think we have a winner in Arts and Crafts. Fergie, that was an excellent poem. And it leaves us in an interesting position. Each finalist in the All-round Frog competition has come first in one of the contests. So whoever wins the last test will be our champion."

"Hop up here, Frog Scouts. Our last test is a spelling contest."

Fergie gulped. He didn't really like spelling words out loud but he got the first word.

"Fergie, spell *tadpole*."

He swallowed and said: "Tadpole: t-a-d-p-o-l-e."

"Webster, spell *toadstool*."

Webster smiled. He loved spelling. "Toadstool. T-o-a-d-s-t-o-o-l."

Roger's word was *gnat*.

"I know. That's easy," he said. "Gnat: n-a-t."

"Oh, I'm sorry, Roger. That's not correct. Fergie, can you spell *gnat*?"

Fergie thought hard. He knew it had four letters, not three. He took a deep breath. "Gnat. K-n-a-t."

"Sorry, Fergie," said Mr. Leatherlips. "That's not correct, either. Webster, do you know? If you do, you're our All-round Frog."

Webster grinned. "Gnat," he said in a clear voice. "G-n-a-t."

"Hooray!" cheered Webster's mother. There was much croaking and flicking of tongues as the frogs greeted the winner.

Back at the swamp, Fergie was sad.

"I wanted to win. I wanted to show you I'm the best little frog in the forest."

"Fergie, no one can be the best at everything," said his father. "But you put heart and soul into every contest. You did your best."

"And you are a wonderful poet," added his mother. "Now come and have some dinner. It's gnat burgers and French flies tonight."

Fergie nodded and then he smiled. "My favourite. Even if I can't spell
    gnat, I can do my best to eat one."
And so he did.

Reflection
Fergie tried his best in that competition,
heart, strength, soul and mind.
He gave all he could
to show that he was a good frog,
a frog to be proud of.

We can try our best every day
to show the world that we are God's people –
good people:
people God is proud of.
I think that's what it means to love God
heart, mind, strength and soul.
We try to do everything for God
and trust that in everything we do,
God's love moves through us
into the world.

But all we can do is try our best.
Sometimes things won't work out the way we wanted.
Sometimes we'll have to try again…and again…and again.
But when we love God,
heart, mind, strength and soul,
God will help us make a difference in the world.

Chant: Chorus and verses 4 and 5.

*(The service continued with the celebration of Holy Communion. At the Abbey,
children are welcome to participate in communion. Because there were many children
present on this occasion, I wrote a responsive format for telling the story of the Last
Supper using questions asked by children. This borrows from the Jewish tradition of
having a child ask questions to remember the significance of the Passover meal.)*

The Story of the Table

Question: What are we going to do at this table?

Answer:
First, we will say a prayer to thank God for everything God has given
    us.
Then, we will break a loaf of bread in pieces
and pass it around the whole church
so everyone who wants to can have a taste.
We will pass these cups of wine around the whole church, too,
so everyone who wants to can have a sip.

Question: Why do we share bread and wine?

Answer:
We share bread and wine today
because Jesus shared bread and wine with his friends long ago.
It was the same night when Jesus was arrested,
on the night before he died.
He asked his friends to keep sharing bread and wine
to remember him.

Question: But I wasn't there with Jesus. What should I remember?

Answer:
When you take a bit of bread,
you should remember that Jesus lived a life like yours.
He shared bread with his friends
and with everyone who needed it.
When you sip the wine,
you should remember that Jesus died because he loves you.
He died to promise you that because God's love is so powerful,
there is nothing to be afraid of, not even dying.

So when we take this bread and this wine,
we remember that Jesus is still with us.

Just as the bread we eat fills our bodies
and the wine we drink warms our hearts,
Jesus fills us and warms us with his love
every day, every place we go.
Now we are going to do as Jesus did.
At table Jesus gave God thanks for the gifts of the earth,
so let us also thank God for everything.

The celebration of communion continues.

Reading between the lines

I have told stories for children as part of worship for many years. *The Adventures of Fergie the Frog* include nearly a hundred stories, each one developed as a reflection on a Bible passage chosen as the theme for the service. The intention in the story is to open up a situation children can recognize from their day-to-day lives and then to explore the feelings associated with the situation in reflection and prayer. Many of the stories have been published and find an enthusiastic response in young children between the ages of four and eight. I would not usually offer a story as the only reflection on the Bible reading for the day but on this occasion, given the theme at the MacLeod Centre, we hoped to model ways of including children in worship and honouring their lives. We worked with the regular elements of Sunday morning liturgy at the Abbey, using a variety of ways to engage young children, things any parish could adapt for its services.

First, we prepared service sheets containing all the words we would use together. This eliminated the frustration of switching from book to book. It certainly used more paper but it allowed us to prepare some sheets in a larger font so that young children (and some older readers, too!) could easily follow the flow of the service. Second, we chose songs with simple words that were repeated – either in a chorus or else as an antiphon or chant. The songs were unfamiliar to many people but had simple melodies. (We recognized after the service we'd used a little too much new music for one service. Still, it is worth remembering that much music familiar to adults is new and strange to children – and often no one stops to teach them how to join in!) Third, we chose to break up the story (which is about the length of sermons I preached in the Abbey) into three segments, each lasting three or four minutes, using a chant between the segments in which the children could stand and sing with hand gestures. The storytellers spoke with comic accents which kept the attention of even the youngest listeners. Most of the children sat close enough so that they could see. Our principles for planning the service tried to honour the biblical text at the heart of the service – offering God heart, mind, soul and strength in worship.

The story reflects something my father said to me when I was a little girl. Whenever I was asked to do something in church – read a lesson, sing a solo verse, take a part in a pageant – he used to comfort and challenge me with these words. "Do your best, Nancy. God deserves your best. But don't worry if it's not *perfect*. God is glad when you do the best you can." As a minister for more than 25 years and as a professor of theology for ten, I've used a version of his wisdom to help others past performance anxiety. When we put our best into whatever we do for God, God will honour our efforts and surprise us.

I had to remind myself of that wisdom when the response to this service emerged over the days and months to follow. There was some deep appreciation – from parents and grandparents who watched their children enter more fully into worship and from a teacher who wanted to use the story to encourage children in other contexts. A few people really liked Mother Frog's description of the soul! But there was also disappointment from adults who expect worship in the Abbey to be an aesthetic experience that will move or comfort them. A very bitter critic complained the service was simply pandering to contemporary society's desire for self-esteem.

As a pastoral theologian concerned with children's spiritual lives, I was deeply saddened by the tone of the criticism. It voiced the kind of expectations that makes much worship alienating to children. A local church may not need to prepare every element of the service to engage the youngest worshippers, as we did this day. Children learn to participate in religious ritual as they become familiar with its patterns. However, if no elements engage those whose reading skills are very basic, many young children and some adults will find themselves unable to join in. And if worship most often relies on our hearing and thinking, then we are denying God the worship offered by all our senses and capacities. Children very often free adults to give heart, strength and soul as well as their minds by responses in worship uncensored by habit or protocol.

4

Justice and Peace Join Hands

It often said that people come to Iona looking for peace and quiet and leave looking for peace and justice. George MacLeod's conviction that worship offered in the church must attend to issues that arise on the streets outside its doors colours the prayers offered in the Abbey day by day. Services of morning prayer lay before God different social concerns that members of the Iona Community are involved in, both locally and internationally. In the years I spent working with the Community, I was deeply impressed by the range of activities members undertook in their local communities, addressing concerns including poverty, literacy, homelessness, human rights and threats to the environment. Many also demonstrated against nuclear weapons held by the British Armed Forces in Scotland. Some members have been willing to go to jail for acts of civil disobedience protesting this threat to the well-being of God's world. Around the Abbey, visitors also notice the silent witness of banners and pamphlets advocating justice on a variety of concerns. Passionate commitment and careful study mark the Iona Community's rule, which guides members in their action for justice and peace.

But prophetic voices make many people uncomfortable. Visitors to the Abbey occasionally take issue with information displayed or the themes for services, arguing that politics have no place in the Church. When a prayer or a reflection disturbs someone, they may protest, thinking that God will never disturb us – especially not in worship. A quick glimpse into Scripture and church history, however, demonstrates that God's Word has often stirred up controversy and deep disagreement. The most painful times have occurred when believers with power and privilege have been challenged to share, to change, to redirect their lives. Iona's prophetic tradition of shaking up the powerful has a long history. I was fascinated to learn about the radical protest in the seventh century by the abbot of the day, Adomnan. He challenged chieftains and church leaders alike to renounce violence against women and children, which was deeply embedded in daily life and social customs of the times. At the Abbey, to continue to raise our voices in protest and in prayer for the well-being of the vulnerable of the earth honours both Celtic Christian insight as well as our biblical heritage.

History, of course, will show us that no one has perfectly clean hands when it comes to justice-making. Therefore, I usually approach a justice issue in worship beginning with its roots in Scripture and reflecting on a contemporary story called forth by the theme. Storytelling lifts up the pathos and complexity of issues, putting real faces on symbols and opinions, inviting deeper reflection. The items in this section demonstrate this approach to storytelling: working with texts assigned for a given day yet wrestling with topics in the news. My goal as a worship leader was not to make people feel bad about what they have done or not done. Rather it was and is to help us look for new angles and new possibilities so that even our small actions can make a mustard seed of difference for God's kingdom.

A double share

Each morning, staff at the island centres hold a brief meeting to co-ordinate the day's activities. Part of that meeting includes a time of sharing headlines from news around the world to keep us up to date. As a Canadian growing familiar with political issues in Scotland and in the United Kingdom, I often chuckled at similarities between Britain and Canada. During my stay, both countries watched long-time prime ministers arm-wrestle their finance ministers over leadership aspirations. Major corporations faced bitter contests between rivals to become CEO. Both the Warden and I were coming to the end of our terms. When the Book of Kings came up in the Sunday lectionary, leadership seemed like a timely topic to consider. This sermon works with 2 Kings 2.9-13 and Luke 9.51-60, texts you may want to read before you have a look at my reflections.

Who will lead the cause once I'm gone?
It's a question politicians struggle with,
especially if they have been around for a while
and their popularity starts to sag.
Those who lead corporations and charities
also have to give some thought to their successors.
Who has both the skill and the vision
to take an organization forward?
As I begin my last few months as deputy warden,
I wonder, too.
Leaders from family business to multinational corporation,
from Scout troop to parish council
have to ask who will take up the mantle
when they step aside.

Not that any of us will be swept up to heaven in a fiery chariot,
as Elijah was.
Elijah's spectacular exit left Elisha holding the mantle of power.
Not that he quite believed he'd get the respect of other prophets the
    way Elijah did.
Like the leader of any political party,
Elisha would have known there'd be some doubters.

So when he struck the sea with the mantle of Elijah,
he cried out in his own doubt and grief –
"Where is the God of Elijah now?"
To his amazement,
the sea parted before him.
It was a sign everyone recognized.
It was the sign of Moses opening the way for God's people.
It was a sign that God's power now rested on him.
Elisha *had* received a double portion of Elijah's spirit.
He was the chosen leader.
There was no doubt.

Many of today's leaders and contenders to the thrones of power
must wish things could be so clear and simple.
If only there was one sign that people recognized
indicating the true spirit of leadership.
In the stories of the Old Testament,
signs of leadership were very important.
In the struggle for power between kings and prophets,
true leaders were known by their miracles.
Not the miracle of a renovated health system
or higher profits for shareholders.
No, Elijah called down fire from heaven
and eliminated his enemies.
Elisha, too, performed miracles
that echoed stories told about Elijah *and* Moses.
Yes, he was a faithful prophet with a double portion of God's spirit
in a time of faithless kings.
He was a leader to be trusted.

Centuries later,
the stories about Elijah and Elisha still influenced people.
Jesus was constantly compared to Elijah.
People wondered if he *was* Elijah,

returned on that chariot to challenge a new generation of faithless
   leaders.
Even Jesus' disciples wondered.
They asked Jesus if they could call down fire from heaven
and burn up a town that refused him hospitality.
"Can we, Jesus? Can we?"
They wanted to use the sign of Elijah
to prove their power over hostile neighbours.
But Jesus rebuked their eager cry to retaliate.

He had to try again to distinguish his way of leading,
to show those who wanted to follow him
what it costs to walk his way.
Jesus began his lesson by refusing to retaliate
against a hostile Samaritan village.
Then he goes on to challenge would-be followers
to risk living an uprooted life,
a life committed to *all* God's people,
not just the people we call family.
He invites people to think outside their familiar framework of home
   and family.
He calls his followers to recognize a new loyalty,
a loyalty that goes deeper even than family relationships –
a loyalty that identifies with God's purposes
to redeem the outcast and stranger.
Jesus expects his followers to build a kingdom where enemies are
   reconciled;
where mercy,
not retaliation,
has the last word.

As Luke tells it in chapter four of his Gospel,
Jesus did claim an inheritance from Elijah and Elisha
at the very beginning of his ministry.
He reminded his hometown friends and neighbours

that these two honourable prophets performed miracles
for *foreigners*.
They used God's power to save desperate people
considered to be *outside* the boundaries of God's love.
Jesus proclaimed *this* radical challenge
as the foundation of *his* ministry:
charity *does not* begin at home.
No, God's charity will search the furthest horizon
for lives in need and opportunities to serve.
If we are to follow such a leader,
we need a double portion of Jesus' spirit –
for hearts can falter when we face the wideness of God's mercy.

Late one evening
I arrived back in Vancouver,
my plane more than an hour late.
Eager to get home, I hurried to my car in the multi-storey car park at
    the airport.
It was almost deserted.
As I turned the key in the ignition, nothing happened.
My heart sank.
I realized the passenger door was ajar.
The interior light had remained on during my trip,
completely draining the battery.
Fear and frustration rose in me.
I looked around in desperation.
A short distance away, I saw a young man,
a cleaner on the airport staff.
I ran over to him to ask where I could find a phone.
In a gracious Punjabi accent, he said,
"Miss, it will cost you much money
to call for help to come in here.
Wait. I will find some friends."
He disappeared and I waited helplessly,

wondering what I should do.

Sure enough, a few minutes later,

a car appeared,

full of Sikh men, wearing turbans and airport security badges.

In Canadian airports,

it is often Sikh immigrants who will work in the rather low-paid
labouring jobs.

These men had had a long day

but they happily pulled up alongside my car.

They spent about ten minutes finding the right cables

to bring my sorry battery back to life.

I was so grateful,

I asked the driver if I could give him some money for their trouble.

"Miss," he said, in the kindest way,

"it is our honour to help you."

It is our honour to help you.

As I drove home,

I thought about my Sikh good Samaritans,

so willing to help a stranger in need at the end of a long day.

I had to ask myself if I would have done the same thing,

if the shoe were on the other foot.

I hope so,

but you know,

I can't say for sure.

Neighbours who are so different from me

easily seem to be a threat,

especially in an inconvenient place

at an inconvenient time.

But my good neighbour said,

"It is our honour to help you."

Elisha wanted a double portion of Elijah's spirit

to become a trusted leader.

We will need a double portion of Jesus' spirit
to become his trusted followers –
so that *we* can find honour reaching out beyond *our* familiar
    connections
to create communities where help is at hand,
no matter who needs it.

This a time when calling down fire from heaven on one's enemies
seems to find favour with many world leaders.
It is a time when fear drives us inward
with a desire to stay close to people who are like us.
In times like *this*,
we need a double portion of Jesus' spirit
if we would come and follow him.
The Good News is this:
he has poured out his Spirit on us
to give us the gifts we need for the work of God's kingdom.
The question is this:
Who will dare
to follow *this* leader?

Reading between the lines

Choosing a text for a Sunday sermon is not always easy. At Iona Abbey,
we usually consulted *The Revised Common Lectionary*, to choose one or two
of the readings being used that Sunday by many churches throughout
the world. But because preachers at the Abbey have the freedom to
choose their own biblical texts, and because the congregation varies
week by week, it is often hard to work with the lectionary. You cannot
assume that listeners will have heard the readings from the previous
Sunday. When the lectionary uses a long story over several Sundays,
a preacher at the Abbey often picks up that story with people who
missed the earlier episodes.

For this particular Sunday, the lectionary reading from the Old Testament was part of the story cycle about the prophets Elijah and Elisha. Their stories were being told over several successive Sundays. Now, from my childhood, I could remember learning the dramatic miracles performed by these prophets. Yet I knew that few of my listeners would know many, if any, of these stories. As I studied 2 Kings, I wondered how to connect its peculiar vision of Elijah's fiery chariot and Elisha's bumbling miracle with my listeners. If they had not heard the dramatic stories about Elijah's miracles on preceding Sundays, Elisha's request for a double portion of Elijah's spirit wouldn't mean very much. I decided to look at the Gospel reading for the day instead. Stories about Jesus were likely to be more familiar to visitors, or so I thought!

When I began to study chapter nine in Luke's Gospel, however, I discovered connections between Jesus and Elijah that I had never noticed before. The more I looked into Luke, the more I realized I had to take this connection seriously. Luke used the figure of Elijah to show us something crucial about Jesus. Whenever I learn something new in my research into Scripture, I figure it is worth sharing in a sermon – as long as I can do so without turning my sermon into a college lecture! As I thought about the ways in which Luke both relates Jesus to Elijah and yet distinguishes them, I began to think about all the leadership contests in the news around me. Politicians in many countries and in different political parties were struggling to distinguish themselves from one another. Large corporations were arguing about who would lead their companies through challenging economic seas. Around me on Iona, several positions on the resident staff were being advertised and interview panels formed. Tests of leadership and loyalty seemed as timely now as they were in the pages of 2 Kings and Luke 9.

Our leadership struggles these days are so different from the miraculous testimonies to Elijah and Elisha. Each miracle proclaimed to followers and opponents alike that God was on the side of these fierce men who challenged the status quo. But today, we grow tired of miraculous promises from politicians. Here, I thought, was our connection with Jesus, who refused to claim Elijah's mantle. He would not call down fire from heaven to incinerate the town that rejected him and his disciples. His refusal to retaliate was a timely symbol as debate over the war in Iraq and its fiery consequences heated up. In Luke's vignettes, Jesus kept inviting followers to choose a deeper loyalty than the one owed to their own flesh and blood. This, too, seemed a timely symbol to consider in the face of growing controversy over immigration in Britain. Yet as a Canadian, I knew much more about how immigration works out in Canada than in Britain. So rather than make a comment on British policy, I thought about my experience in Canada with people whose ethnic and religious roots are very different than mine. The story I told was one in which I felt myself judged and challenged by the surprising kindness of strangers – who were also my neighbours in the most biblical sense of that term. I imagine those who offered to follow Jesus were just as surprised and challenged by his response.

I received two quite different expressions of appreciation for this sermon. Someone who was also very familiar with these stories shared the surprise I had felt while preparing the sermon. He had never before noticed the relationship between Elijah and Jesus in Luke's Gospel. He was delighted to see something "new." However, another listener explained that she hadn't been attending church for very long. She'd never heard these stories before. When she heard the Old Testament reading, she confessed she was completely confused! What a relief, she said, when the sermon helped her make sense of peculiar miracles and odd ancient customs. These comments remind me that there is still a thirst for the wisdom woven through the stories of Scripture, shared by the well-acquainted and the newcomer alike. Interpreting this wisdom as a challenge relevant to our own times is still worthy work for the preacher. By doing the work, she will discover there is always something new to notice in God's Word!

The widow's might

Once a year, members of the Iona Community gather on the Isle of Iona for Community Week, an opportunity to think and talk together about the priorities and commitments of their network. Continuing members recommit themselves to the life of the Community and new members are blessed as they make a public commitment to the Community's rule. During my last season on Iona, I was given the opportunity to preach at the communion service on the day when members made their commitments. Given the Community's long-standing work with and for people struggling against poverty, it was appropriate that both these services fell on the United Nations Day for the Eradication of Poverty. The lectionary text for that Sunday was Luke 18.1-8, the parable of the widow and the judge, a great text to open up concern for the welfare of the poor and the complexities of justice making. I have included the Gospel text using alternate translations of key words that clarify the intended impact of the story. The song used during the reflection, *Ka mana 'o I 'o*, is a gentle melody from Hawaii. It is taken from *One is the Body: Songs of Unity and Diversity* (John L. Bell, ed. © 2002 The Wild Goose Resource Group). Its theme, the faithfulness of God, beats at the heart of the story. The second chant is taken from *Come All You People*, edited by John Bell (© 1994 Wild Goose Resource Group).

A reading from Luke 18 – adapted from the NRSV

Jesus told them a parable about their need to pray always and not to lose heart. He said:

In a certain city there was a judge who neither feared God nor had respect for people. In the city there was a widow who kept coming to him and saying, "Grant me justice against my opponent." For a while he refused; but later he said to himself, "Though I have no fear of God and no respect for anyone, yet because this widow keeps coming at me, I will grant her justice so that she may not finally come and give me a black eye."

A dialogue for two voices:

Peter: Jesus?

Jesus: Yes, Peter?

Peter: She wouldn't really have given him a black eye, would she?

Jesus: Peter, it was just a story to make a point.

Peter: But that widow sounds like she stepped out of the boxing ring. She was giving the judge a hard time. A pretty fierce woman, if you ask me.

Jesus: Peter, do you have a problem with fierce women?

Peter: Well…

Jesus: Peter, have you fallen out with your mother-in-law again?

Peter: Jesus, she's at me all the time. Asking me to help her friends; get them a few extra fish from the boat. Go over and fix a roof. Chop some wood. On my time off.

Jesus: Peter, your mother-in-law is a widow, right?

Peter: Yes, for more than ten years.

Jesus: Are her friends widowed, too?

Peter: Yes, most of them, I think.

Jesus: What does the law teach us about widows?

Peter: *(a little pause)* To look after them. To see they have enough to live on.

Jesus: Right.

Peter: But can't someone else see to them? I need my day off.

Jesus: Peter, when your roof is leaking, does the rain take a day off? When you're hungry, does your stomach take a day off?

Peter: No days off in the kingdom of God, then?

Jesus: Peter, if you need a day off, then send James to fix your mother-in-law's roof. Let John take a fresh fish to her friend. Love will always find a way to get something done.

Peter: Like that fierce little widow in your story?

Jesus: Yes. Just like that fierce little widow your mother-in-law. These
        widows have great faith. They never give up. And they get
        things done – for love's sake.

Peter: …I'd better go patch the roof.

Refrain #1

The reading concludes unannounced:

Listen to what the unjust judge says. Will not God grant justice to his chosen ones who cry to him day and night? Will he delay long in helping them? I tell you, he will quickly grant justice to them. And yet, when the Son of Man comes, will he find faith on earth?

The dialogue continues with the same two voices:

Peter: Jesus?

Jesus: Yes, Peter?

Peter: I don't get it.

Jesus: Get what, Peter?

Peter: Why you asked people to listen to the unjust judge. Is God like an unjust judge?

Jesus: No, Peter.

Peter: Why listen to the judge, then?

Jesus: If you listen to the judge, you'll hear your own heart. You'll see that justice is delayed when people have no regard for each other. When people forget the law.

Peter: Like when I delayed fixing that roof.

Jesus: If the shoe fits, Peter…

Peter: If God isn't like an unjust judge, then is God like…uh…like a…

Jesus: Is God like a feisty widow? Yes, Peter, God is like that feisty widow who didn't give up. God keeps knocking on the door of your heart until you wake up and see what needs to be done.

Peter: Jesus?

Jesus: Yes, Peter?

Peter: When the Son of Man comes, do you think he will find faith on earth?

Jesus: God will not give up on us. God will keep knocking at your heart until you open the door. Uh…Peter?

Peter: Yes, Jesus?

Jesus: Where are you going?

Peter: I just remembered my mother-in-law's neighbour has a door that's falling off its hinge.

Refrain #1

The widows of my first parish taught me how to read this parable.
There was Maisie, 83 the day I met her,
the day after she wallpapered the rooms on the top floor of her house;
86 the day she died,
the day after she brought lumber home from the hardware store to put up shelves
for the preserves she'd made the day before.
Maisie always had a twinkle in her eye
and shortbread in her cupboard for the minister
though her husband had died in his grain field more than 20 years earlier.
She had only herself – and the village – to look after.
Maisie always had a wisecrack
to show me the truth about village life in a loving, laughing way.

Then there was Lena,
who at 79 tore up and down the country roads in a sports car;
whose quiet generosity filled the needs of neighbours
who never knew the gifts came from her.

She nursed her husband through several seasons of senility
long before anyone knew something was wrong.

And there was Faith, parish organizer par excellence,
who'd spot a newcomer at the door of the church
and have a visit planned before they'd opened a hymn book.
Faith never had the chance to enjoy retirement with her husband,
who died shortly after they uprooted themselves to settle in a new part
    of Canada.

Life had scored against these widows,
taking away their dearly beloved partners too soon.
Yet these women were feisty in their faithfulness –
to God and to neighbour.
Good humoured, generous and wise, always welcoming to friend or
    stranger.
But they stand out in my memories of feisty widows
because they had another thing in common.
They had each lost a child, too –
an adult child,
a cherished symbol of their love and their hope.
Their hearts were widowed twice over.

If anyone could lose heart,
could give up on God or goodness,
surely these women had reason.
And yet,
and yet they remained faithful –
faithful to their commitment to help others;
faithful in prayer for anyone in need;
faithful in their insistence that they could –
that *we can* make a difference –
through love that will not give up.

God, whose own heart was widowed in the death of a dearly beloved
    son,
is faithful to the feisty widows.
For God's love is as persistent,
as determined
as bold
as the widow who kept hammering on the conscience of that uncaring
    judge.
Until he did the just thing.
God has not turned a deaf ear to our pleas.
God cries out for the release of an innocent hostage.
God insists we pay attention to suffering
in nations that plead for our compassion
and in neighbourhoods tired out by their struggles.
Our God keeps coming to us like a feisty widow,
to knock at the door of our hearts
and remind us that there is much we can do
to bring justice to lives that cry out to us
for love's sake.

Refrain #1

A prayer for the elimination of poverty:

This night, O God, we surrender our spirits to you and offer all that
    lies on our hearts...

We lift in shame before you the injustice and inequality of our
    world:
a world in which the rich get richer and the poor get poorer,
a world in which the rich judges make the rules
and the poor widows have to live by them;
a world in which the worth of a person is measured by where they
    were born.

Refrain #2

Through our lives and— by our prayers,— your— King - dom come.—

We offer you our longing for peace:
for peace that grows out of the reconciliation of enemies;
for peace that releases resources for human need;
for peace that provides the soil for human flourishing.

Refrain #2

We pray tonight especially for an end to poverty:
poverty that condemns people to disease and early death;
poverty that breeds crime and violence,
    nationally and internationally;
poverty that need not be in a world where there is enough for all.

Refrain #2

We long for a world in which we are all included in the feast of life,
and tonight we remember our unity with those who have lived in
    hope
and died in the service of your kingdom.

(Pause)

Refrain #2

All this we surrender to you, to hold, to heal, to honour with your
    wisdom and mercy,
in the transforming name of Jesus Christ.

Reading between the lines

My fascination with this story began years ago when I was preparing a sermon for the theological school where I used to teach. Preaching before professors and theological students can be a daunting task, given the presence of scholars who know much more about biblical language and history than I do! I did some careful study of this text that led to an insight based on the very unusual language the judge used to describe the widow. He chose the colourful language of the boxing ring to picture her insistence that he pay attention to her claims. In this story, Jesus argues from the lesser to the greater: If something is true in a small example, then this same truth will hold much more firmly in an important example. If something good can be said of a heartless judge, how much more will this goodness hold for God, who is not heartless. This kind of argument is common to ancient storytellers as well as politicians and philosophers. Jesus used it on more than one occasion. As I thought about this kind of argument, I decided to apply it in a different way to the story – to argue from the lesser figure of the widow to a greater truth about God. It seems to me that the story, with its colourful language, points to the widow as the more unusual character. I often look for hidden biblical truth in the more unusual features of a story.

As soon as I allowed the widow to speak for the truth about God, the story and its question about finding faith on earth came into sharper focus. Widows have taught me so much about faithfulness and the courage of the heart needed to persist in goodness and generosity against all odds. The examples I used are a small sample of the wonderful witness I continue to meet in widowed lives that sparkle with love even when tears glisten in eyes that remember the costliness of loss. On Iona I met many such people, too – and I heard stories about many more after I offered this reflection in the Abbey. The widow embodies a deep truth about God. God is persistent in calling out to us to respond in justice and compassion. God is faithful even when we are not. God will not give up on human hearts, whether our resistance arises from a lack of respect for others – as in the case of the judge – or because sorrow has too deep a hold on us – as in the case of many widowed hearts.

For the service, I adapted the translation from the NRSV, inserting its marginal translation, which uses boxing language, in place of its preferred polite version. (Biblical translators seem to struggle with feisty widows as much as Peter did!) I developed the more light-hearted dialogue between Jesus and Peter to present the fruits of my biblical research so that people had time to make the shift in perspective to focus on the widow. The reflection then took us to the heart of the matter. The chant allowed the message to sink in deeply: God is faithful even when circumstances score against us. There *will* be faith on earth because *God* is faithful.

This conviction touched a lot of hearts among Community members who themselves try to remain faithful to the struggle against poverty in the face of many odds. A lot of members work "at the coal face," as they say in Scotland, in local networks to empower those in poverty to claim the dignity and resources they need to make change. Many more work for systemic change, nationally and internationally, especially through commitments for fair trade with small producers around the world and for cancellation of international debt. At every level, the struggle against poverty takes faithfulness, the kind of faithfulness the feisty widow demonstrates. The prayer that follows the reflection was written by my colleague Richard Sharples, Warden of Iona Abbey. It cries out with the widow's passion for God to hear us in our struggles and to support those who suffer most keenly. I believe it is God who opens our hearts to cry out. Therefore, we can be assured God will never abandon us in our commitment to make a difference on behalf of the vulnerable, wherever we encounter each other.

It's just that easy

Iona Abbey is not the only place for worship on the island. Among a number of Christian centres you will find Iona Parish Church, part of the Church of Scotland. There has been a parish church on the island almost as long as the Abbey has been standing. One of the earlier buildings stands in a restful ruin in the garden of the Nunnery. The current parish church occupies a field part way between the Abbey grounds and the heart of the village. There is a commitment among all centres for worship to co-ordinate our services so that our times do not overlap. The parish service takes places at midday on Sunday, after the service in the Abbey has finished. In the winter, the Abbey is too cold for comfort and the weather too stormy to welcome many guests regularly. Therefore, Iona Community staff members join the parish church congregation to worship on winter Sundays. That is how I came to preach on the parable of the sheep and the goats, the assigned reading for the last Sunday of the Christian year, the Sunday marking the Reign of Christ.

The parable of the sheep and the goats
isn't a typical parable.
There isn't much of a story to follow, like we find in the Good
    Samaritan.
Jesus didn't pick on a familiar activity,
like sweeping the house or sowing seeds,
to teach us something about God's kingdom.
The king's decision to separate the sheep from the goats
conjures up the final judgment for us,
a decision by God to weed out worthy souls from the rascals and rotters
    in their midst.
Still, the image in this parable shares something with other parables.
It offers a surprise.
Those goats, those rascals and rotters unworthy of a place in the
    kingdom,
are completely surprised to be told that they have let the king down.

This is really an uncomfortable thought, if you dwell on it.
Shouldn't we *know*,

or at least have a twinge of conscience,
if we have been disobeying God's will?
Aren't the goats of this world *aware*
that their head-butting and voracious appetites and destructive attacks
    on gardens –
don't goats realize *all this* has earned them God's displeasure?

However, I learned something interesting about this parable
that gave me a little different angle on those goats.
I read somewhere that in Jesus' day,
you really couldn't tell a sheep from a goat just by looking.
The varieties of sheep and goats that grazed in the desert looked very
    nearly the same.
Palestinian lambs were not the woolly wee beasts
that leap over Iona's grassy landscapes in spring.
Sheep, like goats, had tough and hairy hides
to ward off vicious sand storms on desolate desert hills.
So the king gathers creatures that all look much the same –
and his measure of judgment surprises all of them.

Like all the parables of judgment, this one is *meant* to make us
    uncomfortable.

"Lord, when was it that we saw *you* hungry or thirsty
or a stranger or naked or sick or in prison,
And did not take care of *you*?"

The king has an answer.
"Truly I tell you,
just as you did not do it to one of the least of these,
you did not do it to me."

These are challenging words.
Anyone who has visited a big city anywhere in the world
has likely walked past at least one outstretched hand.

In city churches where I've worked, we usually had a policy to guide
    our choices
about whom we'd help and how we'd help them.
We'd study those asking for a handout and try to discern who was
    really hungry
and who wanted money for alcohol or drugs
or some other habit we didn't want to encourage.
Based on our experience and our reading of the moment, we made
    choices.
I know I have.
I know I will.
And when I do,
somewhere in the back of my mind I hear the king saying to me,
"Truly I tell you…"
This parable always reminds me of what I *haven't* done.
And you know,
it gets my goat!

But really, it shouldn't.
Let me take you back more than 20 years to my first parish.
I was fresh out of training for ministry, in my early 20s.
I was minister of three small congregations
in tiny Canadian villages with roots back in the time of the Highland
    clearances,
not all that different from this village.
People were so kind to me in my youthful enthusiasm.
I loved to lead Bible study because I had learned so much in my
    training,
so much that helped me make sense of stories I'd learned as a child.
I just wanted to share what I'd learned.
And people came.
On a winter evening we often had 20 or 30 folks
who'd brave their way in the snow for Bible study.
I remember very clearly a Bible study on parables.

I'd done a course in college on parables.

And so I came through the snow,

armed with interesting information about the background to familiar
parables,

about Greek words and text comparisons.

I was *so* ready for this Bible study.

One night we looked at the sheep and the goats.

And I said to my parishioners some of what I've said just now.

This is a parable that makes me feel bad.

It makes me remember every outstretched hand I've walked past.

It leaves me feeling guilty.

It leaves me feeling like a goat.

Then one of the elders raised his hand.

Ian was a humble man,

a farmer with a second job just to keep things going for his family.

He didn't go very far in school

but he was the most conscientious elder I ever worked with.

Ian raised his hand and said,

"Excuse me, Nancy. I don't think this parable is such bad news.

It really is good news.

It tells us just how easy it is to serve Jesus.

The world is full of hungry people, lonely people and sick people.

Any time we want, we can help one of them.

Any time we want, we can help Jesus.

It's just that easy."

Those were Ian's words.

"It's just that easy."

His point was so important, and even so *simple*,

that I felt sheepish.

He made it so clear that I never forgot what he said.

Any time we want, we can serve Jesus.

Any place we find ourselves, we can meet Jesus.

Whenever a stranger finds a welcome smile.
Whenever a hungry mouth is fed.
Whenever a cold body is warmed.
Whenever a sick person is cheered.
Whenever a troubled life is befriended.
It is just that easy to meet Jesus,
to serve Jesus in the lives that bump up against ours.

Likely we have all felt like a goat at one time or another,
knowing we couldn't muster a welcome or a visit
or a bit of generosity to some person in need.
We've been in the crowd on the king's left hand.
"Lord, was it you I frowned at? Was it you I ignored?
     If only I'd known."

(Here, I walked out into the congregation and physically turned around, putting those who had been on my left-hand side when I was facing them on my right-hand as I faced the other way.)

Yet when the king turns around and looks at us from another angle,
he will see us amid the flock on his right hand,
the sheep of his pasture.
He will also see us find the kindness and patience
to welcome yet another stranger to this little island,
to risk a handout for the desperate person calling for our attention,
or sparing some time to visit with a lonely neighbour.

When we follow our best instincts,
when generosity flows from our hearts and hands,
we find the face of Jesus, our king, smiling through each life we risk
     touching.
So every day, try to remember Ian's advice.
Every day remind yourself:
It is just that easy to serve Jesus.
He is standing all around you.

Right beside you.
Reach out.
Offer your hand.
It is just that easy.

Reading between the lines

I felt quite at home in Iona Parish Church. I grew up in small
congregations of the Presbyterian Church in Canada with roots watered
by the historical currents that shaped the Church of Scotland. My
mother's family came to Canada from Scotland nearly 200 years ago,
in the time of the Highland clearances. The first Canadian parish I
served was filled with similar Canadians of Scottish descent. The names
of my friends there are sprinkled along the west coast of Scotland
and across Iona itself. My parish included both a farming area and a
popular tourist region. Its dynamics resonate with the rhythm of life
on Iona – a summer filled with visitors who come and go, followed by
a winter of quiet evenings around the fire when the winds are raging.
I was glad to offer my experience as a preacher to the parish church
on occasion, especially during a winter when the parish had no settled
minister of its own.

When I looked up the Bible reading for the Sunday I volunteered to
preach, I smiled. Matthew's telling of the parable of the sheep and
the goats is one we draw on quite a bit at the Abbey. We lead prayers
for peace and justice on behalf of the Iona Community at least once
a week, and in the heart of the season once a day. The challenge in
this parable is one we draw on to remind people living privileged lives
– ourselves included – that we encounter Christ himself when we will
risk ourselves to care for those who lack basic resources for a dignified
life. This parable is a touchstone for Christian compassion. It leaves
us with no excuse to ignore a sister or brother in need.

Still, parables of judgment do not rest easily with many Christians
whose conscience for social justice is strong. We may be ready to judge

the ethics of government policy or corporate practice when poor people are affected. But commending the goats of this world into the outer darkness of the next world is quite another matter! The theme of God's judgment, wherever it is expressed in Scripture, is sure to make us uncomfortable. As the sermon rehearses, this parable has made me uncomfortable for many years. It still does, for I still face awkward choices of when and how to help people in need. I thought that sharing my discomfort might help us reflect on the parable without turning a judgmental eye on easy targets – those impersonal policies and practices that surrender the interests of the most vulnerable to a self-serving sense of the greater good. We all need to dwell in the discomfort for a while!

I needn't retell the story at the heart of the sermon. The wisdom of this man who would never have thought himself wise has remained with me for more than 20 years, through all the advanced studies and academic roles I've undertaken. He embodies the meaning of "elder" for me. I felt it was important to honour his wisdom in western Scotland, where his ancestors originated. By telling the story of a man they could identify with, I also wanted to honour the wisdom of Iona's local people, who face the same economic challenges that Ian did, combining farming with several other kinds of work to keep things going. The parable isn't really addressing government policies and corporate practices. It speaks to hearts that can offer hospitality. And in small villages and farming communities, sometimes overwhelmed by tourists who find them quaint, Highland hearts do offer hospitality. I know. I've been a lonely stranger in their midst. They have taken me in. This parable assures us that for every opportunity we may have missed, God provides another occasion to respond. It is not about scorekeeping. It is an invitation to open our eyes and see how easy it is to make a difference for someone on the margins.

Just friends

> Once the tourist season moves into high gear, about the beginning of
> June, one more service is added to the daily schedule at the Abbey.
> At 2 p.m., Monday through Saturday, one member of staff leads a
> brief time of prayer and reflection about a justice issue or the need for
> peace in the world. Visitors to the Abbey are invited to interrupt their
> tours and join in for just ten or fifteen minutes. In this way, the Iona
> Community lifts before eclectic groups a wide variety of concerns,
> both global and local. Sometimes people stay out of courtesy; some
> walk out in the middle. Others stay and listen intently, joining in
> prayers found in *The Iona Abbey Worship Book.* When I led these services,
> I tried to tell stories to put a human face on issues and statistics.
> Reflecting on Leviticus 19.17-18, 33-34, this service considers what it
> means to welcome a stranger in our time.

"Will you come to the party? At my house on Friday."
I paused and then went on. "You'll know lots of people. Please come."
  My voice was sincere in its pleading.
Ernesto smiled sadly. "Nancy, I am a refugee. Here in Canada, refugees
  are your *project*. We are not your friends."
I was taken aback. We had worked alongside each other for a few
  months. Ernesto came from El Salvador. He'd been in Canada long
  enough to have secure status and a work permit. He worked with a
  church-sponsored human rights committee. We knew many of the
  same people. But he was right. We were not friends.

Ernesto's comment made me reflect on what it means
to offer welcome
to people who seek refuge in our homelands.
Ernesto had left behind death squads and death threats.
No doubt some of his friends had laid down their lives for truth and
  for justice.
In Canada he was safe.
And he was lonely.
What does it mean to welcome someone like Ernesto?
Not only to share passion about the injustice that hurled them into
  our midst.

Not only to believe in principle
that countries like Canada and Britain ought to welcome those whose
    lives are at risk.
What does it mean to share the give and take,
the risk and the trust,
the insignificant details as well as the common ventures of
    friendship?
It takes more than an invitation to a party.

Ernesto didn't come to my party.
His words still haunt me.
Every time I hear a debate about asylum-seekers –
what "they" want in "our" countries –
I think of his words,
offered in simple recognition, not accusation.
Injustice continues for Ernesto as long as he is known by that label,
refugee,
asylum-seeker,
and not as friend and neighbour.
Today marks one year since a Kurdish asylum-seeker was murdered
    in Scotland.
He was beaten
and he died
in a neighbourhood where he thought he would find safety
and a new home.
It is an important day to consider the teaching of the law and the
    prophets,
teaching that Jesus himself affirmed.
People who honour God are called to honour each other
no matter where we come from,
how we differ from each other and what our plight.
We are called to make a place for one another in our lives
and to care for each other from our substance.

There are 388,000 people seeking asylum in the European Union this year;
    approximately 80,000 of those individuals seek refuge in the United
    Kingdom.
Today I invite you to consider how many,
if any,
of those people are your neighbours and friends.
When we know someone as friend and neighbour,
the story of their situation is not a statistic.
It is a testimony of God's concern.

Let us pray:
Jesus, friend of strangers and outsiders,
how did you do it?
How did you find the energy, the understanding,
how did you take the risk
to open yourself to people who came from unfamiliar places,
who carried stories beyond your own experience?
Why did such people find such safety in you
that they opened their hearts to you?
Can we take the risk, too?
Today we pray for refugees and asylum-seekers,
those taking shelter in our homelands
and those desperate to get away from persecution...

When they leave everything familiar behind,
help them find welcome and security in new places, among new
    neighbours.
When we meet such folks,
give us a heart for their stories
and wisdom and generosity to help them build their futures
as our friends and neighbours.
Amen.

Reading between the lines

My encounters with people who came to Canada as refugees began when I was a young parish minister. The denomination I belong to was part of an ecumenical effort to provide safe homes and a new beginning for people who set sail from Vietnam in very leaky boats. In my small parish, opinions differed deeply. Some people were glad to help, generous in what they contributed. Others were deeply suspicious. Only a few were willing to meet the family who came to our area and struggle over barriers of language and culture to welcome them face to face. Since that time, I've met and worked with people who escaped from many different places – Argentina, Guatemala, Chile, Colombia, South Africa, Iran, Burma, Sri Lanka. Even this short list calls to mind several decades of political struggle and persecution. Some of those countries are safer now; some are not. The testimony of these witnesses still needs to be heard to remind us all what can happen when power becomes corrupt.

My own family's roots in Scotland and the story of the Highland clearances helped me understand why I feel so passionately about the duty I owe to those who must flee their homelands. From the late eighteenth century through the middle of the nineteenth century, thousands and thousands of people were "cleared" from western Scotland. For reasons that were partly political and partly economic and always about power, families who had eked out an existence for generations in this part of Scotland, Iona included, suddenly found themselves squeezed into ill-prepared cities or thrust onto boats headed out to sea. Many of those boats landed on the east coast of Canada: among their passengers were my great-great-grandparents. Those new "Canadians" did not have an easy time building new lives. Their fledgling settlements often displaced aboriginal communities with many unhappy consequences, especially for native well-being. In contemporary debates about asylum rights and economic need, I often reflect on the complex connections between Scotland and Canada. The tragedies on both sides of the ocean created an unanticipated legacy of families broken in so many different ways. In Scotland, even as a temporary resident, I felt well and truly welcomed. As both guest and host on Iona, I began to ask myself how I can become a better friend to the newcomers I meet wherever I live.

Over the years, I've been in my share of debates about refugee policy. So many people judge *all* refugees by the stories of a few who abuse the system while trying to establish their claim. Yet, even when we are supportive of asylum policies and willing to welcome those in genuine need, relationships take time to build. Customs and cultures are so different. Terror destroys trust, which is not quickly replaced. In telling this story, I wanted to put a responsible face on the term "refugee" – and also to acknowledge that even the most sympathetic among us have to work carefully and consistently to bring those who come as strangers into full partnership in our neighbourhoods and networks. Community is a lifetime commitment.

5

Christ of My Own Heart

"What *are* people looking for in the quest for Celtic spirituality these days?"

The question came from an Iona Community member during a discussion at the MacLeod Centre. Our group came up with a list of things often associated with Celtic tradition – the place for nature's voice and beauty, a sense of God's close presence, the intricate lines of art and lilting lines of music, everyday language with poetic cadence. These traits are not unique to Celtic Christian expression, but they combine to give what is often recognized as "Celtic spirituality" a timely appeal.

So many people who come to Iona from large urban areas find themselves refreshed and awakened to wonder when they gaze around the expansive horizon. An experience of wonder, of sensing one's place within a much wider universe, opens up space for God in lives weary of routine demands. To know oneself as part of a larger whole is spiritual truth. Such knowledge creates an awareness of a presence beyond us, a presence of holy proportion. We may begin to respect more deeply other fragile pieces of this whole because we sense our connections to them. Many contemporary spiritual seekers hope that a recovery of Celtic sensibilities will encourage honour for our endangered earth. This longing is born as much from current awareness of threats to the environment as it is from some forgotten wisdom. However, if people are moved to better environmental practice through texts of Celtic prayer, it would be "no bad thing," as some Scots say.

Celtic art and music from different periods and places have become very popular. Scottish, Irish and Welsh folk tunes in contemporary arrangements lift spirits in the Abbey these days, but rarely the awesome drone of Columban chant. Still, folk tunes have often done double duty in Christian circles, carrying both sacred and secular songs of the heart. Typical designs in Celtic art symbolize core convictions of Celtic Christian faith, although the meanings may need some interpretation. For example, the unending lines that weave in and out of intricate knots are said to represent God's eternal presence. Perhaps the symmetry and grace created by Iona's weavers and silversmiths, past and present, renew this promise to help us make sense of tangled lives. Celtic monasteries had a central role in preserving these arts during centuries of turmoil through their painstaking work to copy and illustrate Biblical manuscripts. Iona was also home to a school of stone-carving whose trademark designs can be found on crosses still standing throughout Scotland. Here is subtle testimony to God's purposes at work in human creativity even when those purposes become clear only in "holy hindsight."

In our discussion of things Celtic that day, however, I decided to put forward something else I'd noticed through months of similar conversations: "I think some people are also seeking a spirituality that avoids Jesus." A few eyebrows were raised. I explained what I'd been observing. For example, some worship leaders always chose spoken responses or prayers that claimed the blessing of moon and stars without mentioning the name of Christ. Commitment services often focused on an ethic within the Gospel, but not on the person of Jesus himself. In workshops, we frequently wrestled with questions about who Jesus was and is in a world with so many religious traditions as well as spiritualities with no particular religious root. "Isn't it an offence to such diversity to raise up Jesus' name?" some people argued. "Isn't it more inclusive to speak of God or the Spirit?" Such questions trouble people in this day and age, especially when extreme religious views provoke dangerous conflict.

As far as I can discern, however, these were not questions that puzzled Celtic Christians like Columba and his brothers. For them, Christ stood at the heart of their faith. St. Martin's Cross, erected on Iona around the eleventh century, cradles the Christ child within the distinctive circle at the centre of the cross. Prayers gathered from Highland sources during the nineteenth century call on Jesus as companion in cottage and field, Son of Mary, born for us. In a newer generation with Celtic roots, the Iona Community expresses its Christian faith with a similar emphasis on God's incarnation in Jesus Christ – God "who walks the road of our world's suffering with us," as one Iona communion liturgy puts it. Jesus' example reaching out to those on the margins, those shunned by the "properly" religious, animates worship and action for Community members day by day, providing a model of how to confess his name. Celtic Christian prayer invites us to reclaim Jesus as our daily companion. The Iona Community asks us to include among Jesus' companions those whose experience lies beyond our own.

Spurred on by so many discussions about Jesus, I often chose to reflect on stories from the Gospels in worship. Sometimes, crucial Gospel truth has become obscured by "churchy" terms that people no longer find meaningful. When I preached or celebrated communion at the Abbey, I tried to translate the ancient truths I trust about Jesus into stories and symbols that can speak in today's terms. Christian tradition can actually help us here, because it offers so many different lenses to focus Jesus' love for us – teacher, friend, prophet, servant, truth, light, bread of life. Sometimes, however, people reduce Jesus to a single image or title, which then limits his relationship with us. Eventually we struggle with the very limits we've set for ourselves.

Inapprehensible we know you, Christ beside us, prayed George MacLeod. Whether in the poetry of the Community's founder or the rune prayer

known as St Patrick's Breastplate, Christians of Celtic heritage find
Christ at the heart of things. The five items in this section explore
the implications of faith in Christ for lives in this generation. They
intentionally travel over some traditional "turf" of Christian doctrine,
following less traditional paths in the search for renewed meaning. A
Christmas meditation considers the place of a saviour in a world where
it's hard to admit when something goes wrong. A Lenten sermon faces
the uncomfortable paradox that in dying, we find life. A poem stands
before Jesus on the Cross, considering what it means to suffer "for
us." A resurrection miracle asks us how we remember and want to be
remembered in Jesus' name. Finally, a dialogue built around a parable
of Jesus provokes consideration of the face of God whom we meet in
Christ. As you read my confessions about Jesus, think about what Jesus
is revealing about God's presence and God's power and God's purpose.
These themes are the roots of Celtic Christian faith, as I have come to
appreciate it. These are roots to nourish us all in such a time as this.

To you a child is born

With its familiar carols and traditions both beautiful and banal,
Christmas brings the challenge to find a fresh angle in preaching.
Iona Abbey will welcome to worship a very diverse congregation at
Christmastime. Some people come because they love Christmas on the
island, others because they have chosen to break with family tradition
and seek a refuge from city sparkle. Often, during its Christmas
House Party, the Abbey embraces at least a few guests who are finding
the celebration difficult because of a recent change in personal
circumstances. As I reflected on my task to celebrate communion on
Christmas night with such folks in mind, I recalled an idea introduced
to me many years earlier by an American professor of preaching
and worship, Thomas Troeger. He described a woodcut by Albrecht
Dürer used as a focus for a Christmas homily. I remembered that the
wood cut featured a barn that was falling apart. I went looking for a
copy of the woodcut, knowing that at least a few of those in worship
that night would identify with an image of a world crumbling around
them. As you read the meditation that follows, pause at the point for
the chant and study the drawing for yourself. You might even want to
sing a verse of "Silent Night" in those moments and listen anew to its
convictions about this child.

Voice One: In that region there were shepherds living in the fields,
keeping watch over their flock by night.

Voice Two: An angel of the Lord stood before them and the glory of
the Lord shone around them,

Voice One: and they were terrified.

Voice Two: Do not be afraid; for see – I am bringing you good news
of great joy for all people: to you is born this day in the
city of David a Saviour, who is Christ the Lord. This will
be a sign for you: You will find a child wrapped in bands
of cloth and lying in the manger.

Voice Three: Suddenly there was with the angel a multitude of the heavenly host, praising God and saying,

All three: Glory to God in the highest heaven, and on earth peace, goodwill among people.

Voice Three: When the angels had left them and gone into heaven, the shepherds said to one another,

Voice One: Let us go now to Bethlehem and see this thing that has taken place, which the Lord has made known to us.

Voice Three: So they went with haste and found Mary and Joseph,

Voice Two: and the child lying in a manger.

Voice One: When they saw this, they made known what had been told them about this child

Voice Three: and all who heard it were amazed at what the shepherds told them.

Voice Two: But Mary treasured all these words and pondered them in her heart.

Chant or a verse of a carol for all to sing.

Have a look at the woodcut printed on your service sheet.
The nativity scene was carved in 1511 by an artist named Albrecht Dürer.
Study it for a minute.
What do you notice?

In some ways, the scene is just another picture,
fitting Mary and Joseph with the clothes of its day.
The shepherds look like European peasants, not Middle Eastern herders.
By 1511, European art had achieved some fine moments.

The prints of Albrecht Dürer's woodcuts were regarded
as sophisticated achievement.
This is one of his simpler carvings.
But it shares one feature with all his other nativity scenes.
The world it pictures
is falling apart.
Did you notice?
Did you spot the gaping holes in the barn roof?
See the grass sprouting from the crumbling walls?
In each nativity scene Dürer produced,
Christ is born
into a world that is falling apart.
Those who stoop to welcome the newborn king
don't seem to notice.
But somehow I think it is very important for us to see.
Christ is born for us
because we are all in some way incomplete.
Christ is born into our midst
when it feels like the roof might just fall in.

For many people in 1511, the roof was falling in.
The plague was stalking its victims;
unrest was brewing in church and state.
The high culture that surrounded Albrecht Dürer
had started to come apart at the seams.
And so this artist confesses his faith:
Christ is born –
again and again –
into a world that is falling apart.

Surely it seems some days
that our world is coming apart at the seams.
War and terrorism;
crime and punishment;

illness, hunger, drought and poverty:
everywhere we look.
Is there any doubt our world needs a Saviour?

But our Saviour is not a politician who threatens rogue nations.
Nor a scientist seeking support for some new global solution.
Our Saviour is a baby.

Now, a baby calls out of us the best we have to offer;
the deep concern, the tender smile,
hands willing to clean up a mess.
A baby needs wisdom and patience to help it grow,
and love that won't give up
even when it wears thin on another late night.
Such are the gifts Mary and Joseph offered their child
in a threatening time.
Such are the gifts we have to offer to our children,
to our neighbours,
to earth itself,
when the global roof is threatening to fall in.
Such are the gifts our Saviour needs
to touch the time in which we live with truth and grace.

Chant or verse of a carol

And truly, every one of us here knows
in ways both simple and profound
that the world has a way of falling apart
despite our best intentions and efforts,
despite our faithful confessions and heartfelt prayers.
Is there any doubt that *we* need a Saviour, too?
Not one who argues with us and says
"I told you so."
Not one who frowns at us
and makes us regret that we ever needed to ask for help.

It is good news
that the Saviour who comes to us
when our confidence is leaking
and the cracks in our world fill with tears
is a baby;
One who looks at us with the wonder of a small child seeing
    everything,
everyone for the first time;
One who smiles and reaches for us
because we are who we are.

We are there for the trusting touch of this baby's love.
And this baby called Jesus,
this Saviour,
calls out of each one of us the best we have to offer –
the deep concern that aches within us sometimes;
the tender smile that blesses others in a tired moment;
hands willing to clean up a mess whether or not we were responsible
    for it;
wisdom and patience with ourselves – and with each other –
so that we can grow;
and love that won't give up
even when it feels threadbare.
We can offer what we have,
little though it may seem,
because the love of this baby –
reaching out from the cradle,
reaching out from the cross –
will never let us go.

Chant or verse from a carol

Invitation to communion:

And so it was that Jesus said,
Unless you come like a child
you will not enter the kingdom of God.
Jesus came as a child
to show us that we have a place at God's table.
As a baby,
before he could sit at the table,
Jesus depended on his mother's milk
and her skillful fingers wiping him,
wrapping him,
rocking him.
He depended on Joseph's courage
to keep him safe
and put daily bread on the table.
Can we depend on God's tender fingers
to sort through the knots in our lives
like a mother combing her child's unruly hair?
Will we allow God's strong and gentle arms
to wrap us round with compassion,
even when we squirm for independence?
Can we trust the courage that carried the cross for us,
and live as if that kind of love will never let us go?
God invites all such children
to share this Christmas dinner.
At this table,
let us receive the gifts of bread and wine
as eagerly as children open a Christmas present,
knowing it is for us,
hoping it will change our world.
So let yourself depend on God tonight.
Trust the love that has called you here
and calls you by your name.

Reading between the lines

During my search for a Nativity scene by Albrecht Dürer, I looked through several collections of his work. It turned out that he produced quite a few nativity scenes, both wood carvings and etchings. As I looked for the one Tom Troeger might have had in mind, I noticed that Dürer had used this same artistic feature in each one – the stable or house framing the Christ child is in decay. The 1511 print that I chose drew me in through the figure of the baby. The Christ child is central, yet look at his position. He rests in a slightly awkward pose, reaching out to those around him – as a baby would if it needed a response from an adult. With this picture in mind, I went back to the Christmas story in the Gospel of Luke to consider what that familiar story might say afresh.

The words of the angel that highlight the Christ Child caught and held my attention, just as the position of the baby in the wood carving had. The angel declares to the shepherds: "To you is born this day in the city of David a Saviour, who is Christ the Lord. This will be a sign for you: You will find a child wrapped in bands of cloth and lying in the manger." The angel pronounces the three classic titles we claim for Jesus: Saviour, Christ and Lord. I began to prepare my meditation doing word study on these titles, thinking I would focus briefly on each one in turn. These titles are sung so often in Christmas carols and they say so much about Jesus, but they are so familiar we hardly think about them. Especially at Christmas, the baby Jesus catches our attention. I thought that exploring the titles could draw our thoughts beyond the manger to gifts that Jesus offers when the world is crumbling around us, as the woodcut pictures.

However, as you can tell from the meditation, one title claimed my attention. Saviour. As I began to write, the figure of the baby in the woodcut and the significance of a Saviour in a world that was falling apart seemed like more than enough to draw us together around the Lord's Table. The title of Saviour has a counter-cultural ring in these days of self-help books and personal trainers. When I was teaching students for ministry, I met many who really resisted the notion that humankind needs a saviour. Such people insisted that we are God's good creation, made in God's image, and therefore we can contribute goodness to the world. What we need, they argued, was self-esteem, not salvation, in order to appreciate who we are and what we bring to the community of God's people. Now, of course, there is truth in this argument: God's truth. I believe that God creates us for goodness' sake and that we can contribute good gifts to the life of the world. But this does not replace my trust in the saving grace of Jesus the Christ, whose life touched and restored so many aching lives, whose forgiveness and friendship set so many others on a new path. My world has crumbled often enough to know that I need God's strength and help to go on.

Studying the angel's words and Dürer's print raised a question that became the heart of my Christmas meditation: What does it mean that the Saviour is a baby, a child? I continued to be drawn in by the posture of Dürer's Christ, reaching out, asking us to respond to him. This is the wonder of so many newborns. It is also the gift of the Christ, reaching out to us and asking us to respond, whether we trust our ability to respond or not. I chose to highlight the ways we respond to a newborn child and to connect that response to the ways in which God invites us to respond to the world and its predicaments.

The reading and meditation were designed for an evening communion service at the Abbey when I knew a few young children would be present. The service took place on Christmas night when we had already heard the reading from Luke three times in the preceding 24 hours. To offer a fresh hearing, I divided the short text for three voices and placed the readers around the space in which we gathered so that we had a sense of being held in the story. The voices read only parts of verses, changing when the characters change or the visual focus shifts. (The congregation sang the "Gloria in excelsis Deo," taking the part of the heavenly host.)

After the reading and at key points during the reflection, we paused to sing in response to what we had heard. If the spoken word had touched a heart or nerve, singing could release emotion gently, prayerfully. For this service, we used a song from Brazil, "Um Menino" ("A Child"), with original words and music by Simei Monteiro, English translation by Michael Hawn. Its chorus gracefully emphasizes the wonder in every child and its verses tell of the concerns the Christ child holds for us in a troubled yet wondrous world. It worked very well in a congregation willing and able to take on new music even on Christmas night. I think it would be equally effective to use a familiar carol at these points, singing a verse at a time. "Silent Night" and "Child in a Manger" are carols in which the titles for Jesus are spun around the manger scene in gentle melodies. Using them in dialogue with this meditation would highlight the proclamation in those carols in a fresh way.

For evening communions on Iona, we often sit around a long table laid down the centre aisle of the Abbey. It gives the feel of a dinner table, something I highlighted for the children who had been sitting around Christmas dinner tables only a few hours before. I wrote a new invitation to communion for this occasion with the children in mind. On Iona, we welcome children to the table along with adults from any Christian tradition. I hoped that adults, having experienced the eagerness of children around the Christmas dinner table, might be reminded of the wonder we share in as the gifts of communion are broken open for us.

After the service that night, I was approached by one of our guests who was making his first visit to Iona, a father missing his children in a family that had broken apart. He thanked me for the service, for the way in which Christmas had become transparent for him, allowing him to see God embracing the world and including him again. I believe that Albrecht Dürer would be glad to know his art still proclaims such Good News.

Unless a seed dies

Preaching in Iona Abbey on Sunday morning is an immense privilege – and quite a responsibility. Ever since that stranger spoke to me in the ferry queue about my sermon, I kept occasional visitors to the Abbey in my sights when I was preparing to preach. This sermon is based on John 12.20-33, the text assigned for the two weeks before Easter. For those of us making a deliberate journey through Lent toward the cross, John's language in this passage is code for what we know will happen to Jesus. Still, his code is a challenge. It speaks in paradox – of the *glory* and *honour* of a *servant*; of *losing* one's life in order to *find* it; of seeds *dying* in order to *bear fruit*. Complex symbols for listeners steeped in the parables of Jesus. How could they speak to those who simply dropped into the Abbey that Sunday, to someone unaware that Jesus' journey to the cross had begun? A story came to mind and wouldn't let go.

He came into the church late one November afternoon.
It was pouring rain.
I'd just dashed in to get something from my office,
hoping to make a quick getaway.

"Can I use the phone?"

I looked at him more closely.
A young man, still in school, I thought,
not wearing a coat even in the pouring rain.
Thinking he'd had car trouble, I said,
"Go ahead, if it's a local call."

As he dialled, he glanced around the church.
He chuckled and said,
"Imagine. A Satanist comes to *a church* to call for help."

I swallowed.
A Satanist was using my office phone.
A Satanist stood between me and the door.
A six-foot-tall, strapping young Satanist
had me trapped in my office.

My Hollywood imagination conjured up a scene
as the young man spoke into the phone.
Would unsuspecting members of my congregation
find me sacrificed on the communion table
when they came to clean the church the next morning?
I began to edge toward the door.
This was not the kind of death
I would have chosen for myself.

Today is known as Passion Sunday in many churches.
It is a day to consider the death of Jesus
and its significance for us
as we move closer to the Cross.
Today's reading from the Gospel of John
provides an image of the kind of death Jesus would die,
an image to help us consider
the meaning of our own commitments in life and in death.

John pictures Jesus' death as a sign.
He believes that God is acting to reveal true glory
through Jesus' surrender of himself.
But this is not always the way people view Jesus' death.
Throughout history
and into our own generation,
Jesus' death has been seen as
weakness;
a tragic mistake;
a piece of gruesome history
covered up by rumours of resurrection.

Take my young Satanist, for example.
He was on the phone for quite awhile.
Then he asked if I would come and take the line.
"The youth worker wants to talk to you."
My fear eased a bit.

I found myself speaking with a youth worker in the next city.
He explained he was part of a Christian team
advertised on radio stations that appealed to young people.
"We invite kids who are mixed up in Satanic ritual
to call us if they want to talk.
I'm going to come and talk to Steve.
I'll be there in an hour.
Will you keep him talking until I get there?"
I looked at the young man.
Steve the Satanist.
Somehow I'd imagined a name like Voltan or Draco.
Steve.
He was just 15.
And his mother's boyfriend had hit him in the face.
So he'd run out of the house in the pouring rain without a jacket
and come to the first place he thought he'd find help.
A church.
We sat in the sanctuary and talked as we waited.
Steve picked up a Bible
and flipped through it, glancing at the words.
He stopped when he read: Love your enemies.

"Do you believe that?" he challenged me.
"Yes," I said.
"We believe that love is weak.
You should hate people who push you around.
Look here. It says turn the other cheek.
That's crazy."

As Steve repeated to me some things he'd learned
from what he called the Satanic Bible,
I heard many of the teachings of Jesus turned upside down.
Hate your enemies.
Hit them first.
Whatever else it does,

this movement cannot accept the crazy teachings of Jesus
that insist we serve others and put ourselves last, not first.
Steve was convinced that strength is a master,
not a servant.

But let us listen to Jesus.
" 'Unless a grain of wheat falls into the earth and dies,
it remains just a single grain;
but if it dies, it bears much fruit.
Whoever serves me must follow me.'
He said this to indicate the kind of death he was to die."

A seed must surrender its individual existence
in order to produce its fruit.
A seed gives life by dying to its hard, smooth, perfectly packaged
    beginnings.
When the plant emerges from the soil,
the original seed has disappeared.
It has died to give birth to its crop of fruit,
its blossoms of beauty and the next generation of seed.

Jesus dares his followers to live by this pattern of paradox.
If we dream of life as a perfect package,
smooth, neat,
encased in a solitary shell of home and office arranged for our own
    enjoyment,
we are like seeds that wither on the shelf.
Jesus challenges us
to plant ourselves in the common ground of God's world;
to give our energy-producing goodness
that feeds the goodness of the whole world,
not merely our own desires.

If we love life as a perfect package
and set our hearts on achieving it for ourselves,

Jesus says we will lose it.
We will know only the sterile loneliness
of a seed stuck in its own shell.
But when we die to the desires the world considers important,
when we give ourselves to others, *for* others,
our lives are enriched beyond measure.
It is a promise that only makes sense
once we have taken the risk and committed ourselves
to the messy soil of compassion –
loving our neighbours *and* our enemies.

Our fruitfulness,
our beauty and purpose
are only discovered in the midst of giving ourselves away.
Steve, my young Satanist,
could not understand this.
Instead,
he described sacrificing a bird on the grounds of the church late one
    night.
"I had such a rush of power," he said,
"as I watched it die."
"Didn't you feel anything for the bird?" I asked.
He was silent.
He hadn't considered the bird until that moment.

I looked at him sitting beside me.
A bruise was forming on his cheek.
He was only 15.
He lived with people more concerned for their own interests than
    his.
He had little respect or support in his life.
The only power he could feel
was the rush of his own strength snuffing out a bird's life.

"Steve," I said,

"I can only tell you what I believe.
I believe that love is the only force strong enough
to defeat evil in the world.
I believe that Jesus died for love's sake
and his love inspires us to care for others in every way we can.
Just remember that you came to a church for help on a rainy
  afternoon.
You can come back here if you ever need help again.
That's why we're here.
For Jesus' sake."

I don't know what happened to Steve
because he didn't come back in my time at that church.
I pray for him
whenever I remember our encounter.
And I thank God for youth hotlines and youth workers
who are willing to invest time and energy and love for lives like his,
lives that know so little of hope and generosity;
lives that need some place to turn.

In his life and in his death,
Jesus reversed the values of the world.
Abundant life is not attained by the acquisition of things
or the triumph of force
or by achieving fame and popularity.
Abundant life is the gift God gives us
through the giving of others.
Jesus risked himself,
trusted himself
to the power of love that grows through patient self-giving.
A seed cannot see the results of its growth
when it surrenders itself to the ground.
We will not always see the results of our love
invested in lonely lives
and what seem like lost causes.

But if we would see Jesus,
then we are called to look into the midst of the neighbourhoods
where we are planted.
We are called to spend ourselves,
our time, our understanding, our money
growing relationships with vulnerable people:
with God's fragile world.
When we are rooted in the belief
that God's love produces abundance from tiny grains of generosity
and small seeds of compassion and commitment,
there is no other way to invest our lives.
We are called to be a place to turn.

Jesus died to promise us that God's love
can reverse the powers of death and destruction,
of greed and fear that have such a strong grip on the world.
Jesus committed himself to the fearless and hopeful generosity
held by every grain of wheat.
He died to feed the world with fearless, hopeful generosity
through which the true glory of God shines.
We taste it here in bread and wine.
We can share it wherever we go
if we trust the power of love to grow goodness
with fearless, hopeful generosity
even in the face of death.

Reading between the lines

When I am seeking to explore symbols in worship, I try to find a story
that can draw participants into the many layers of meaning every
symbol holds. The most familiar of the symbols in John's text is the
seed, and so I began my sermon preparation by sifting through my
memory for stories of seeds and growth and fruitfulness. Nothing much
came to mind. I moved on to consider the connection between being
glorified and being a servant. As I mulled over these ideas, the story of

Steve jumped into my mind. I can't explain why. At first, I just noted it on the page of brainstorming I do to start every sermon. It didn't seem to fit the symbol of glory that John's Gospel identifies with Jesus' death. But the episode, which happened more than ten years earlier, kept insisting itself into my plans, so I scrapped the other ideas I was squeezing so hard and outlined what had happened that day.

I remembered the fear I had felt, aware of violent vandalism to neighbouring churches, vandalism filled with satanic symbols. Until Steve appeared in my office, I'd shrugged off the satanic elements of the vandalism because my Christian faith is not fed by fear of dark forces or thoughts of a battle against "the ruler of this world," as John's text says in verse 31. But I did feel a flash of fear for my personal safety that afternoon. I had to overcome that fear in order to stay with the young man who sought refuge in my church. The more I worked with the story of that young man, the more connections I found in the text and in the rich symbols it draws together.

Like so much of Jesus' teaching, John's story is filled with paradox. Reflecting on my conversation with the would-be Satanist, I recalled how little he could grasp the paradox of the Gospel that he read from the Bible that afternoon. I suddenly realized that Steve's struggle might be shared by others who wandered into worship that day. Jesus' love turns the world's symbols of glory upside down. Following Jesus means resisting the temptations of power and glory that lure us to seek our own interests first. Though I doubt people in worship that morning would have read a "Satanic bible" as Steve had, many would surely have struggled with the Gospel's insistence that serving others, resisting revenge and loving enemies form the true path to abundant life. The truth he rejected is a challenge to us all. It was only after I'd preached this sermon that I saw something else in my story. In my conversation with Steve, the so-called ruler of this world had been challenged and an invitation offered to draw this young man to Jesus (verse 32). I could then see why the story insisted on being told as a mirror to John's story.

Listeners responded positively to the story. A number of them identified with my surprise that a self-proclaimed Satanist had an ordinary name and came from a sadly ordinary troubled home. For others, it was an introduction to the notion that Satanic ritual is a reality in suburban settings and something of a surprise to hear it mentioned in Iona Abbey. I could identify with this surprise. Until that rainy afternoon, I'd never met anyone who claimed that term for himself. I'd never heard quotations from a Satanic source. I'd never really given serious thought to the burned-out fires and remains of small birds we'd found in the field beside our church. And I'd never before given a one-to-one confession of faith to a young skeptic the way I did that day. Yet, face to face with Steve, I knew that in his brush with Satanism he'd stumbled into a world that wouldn't bring him life. It only reinforced the abuse of power, an abuse he'd already experienced. I felt I had to show him the possibility God's love held for him. Wherever and whenever I preach, I realize I am giving my face-to-face confession of faith to dozens, even hundreds of people. What I say, I must believe. I must believe that my stories and symbols, my explanations and arguments are rooted in the life-giving, love-bearing soil of the Gospel. And I do trust that even as the seeds of my words die in the ears of my listeners, some will sprout in fruitful contemplation, as the Spirit tends them.

I pray that this is so for Steve's sake and for Christ's sake.

He is crucified

Each year the activities for Holy Week at the island centres involve the preparation of Stations of the Cross. Inspired partly by the traditional themes that have drawn Christians along the Way of the Cross and partly by the creativity of our Easter guests, the Stations involve poetry and prayer, drama and art work to take us through the stories of Jesus' last day. On Good Friday morning, we set up stations along the road that leads from the village to Iona Abbey. A large crowd gathers and walks behind a cross from station to station, each one leading us closer to the moment of crucifixion.

Just before Holy Week 2004, I had seen Mel Gibson's controversial movie *The Passion of the Christ*. I found the graphic violence hard to watch. The brutality while Christ was flogged left me gasping. I shut my eyes when Jesus was nailed to his cross. I left the theatre numb, wondering if I had spent more than 40 years as a Christian in denial of the pain Jesus suffered. When I returned to Iona, I wondered how I could take part in the Stations of the Cross this year. Could I take any more drama? I watched as creative teams were set up to design the Stations. A gap emerged. No one volunteered to prepare the station for the moment when Jesus is crucified. We could hardly skip this part of the story! So I gathered my courage and volunteered. This poem emerged from my reflections.

His body hangs heavy,
the weight of the world
drags his life
from his aching lungs.
His breath surrenders,
gasp by gasp.
What takes his breath away?

Pain.
The staggering pain
inflicted by those terrified of losing face,
losing place,
losing power to run the world
their way.

A black ribbon is tied on one arm of the cross in silence.

Gasp
by gasp,
what takes his breath away?

Fear.
The shuddering fear
that God has no regard;
that we,
that *I* am not good enough;
that this…
is all there is.

A second black ribbon is tied on the other arm of the cross in silence.

Gasp
by
gasp,
what takes his breath away?

Tears.
The suffocating tears
that choke his sorrow,
knowing we are afraid.
Knowing we have not yet grasped
The truth.
The love.
The grace he lived
for us.

A third black ribbon is tied at the foot of the cross in silence.

Gasp

by

gasp,

what takes
his breath
away?

Love.
The all-embracing love
that spreads its arms
to promise us:
This
is enough.
This pain.
This sorrow.
This
gasping
gift
is enough
to give us
life
in all its fullness.

A white bandage is wrapped around the centre of the cross in silence.

His body hangs heavy,
the weight of the world
drags his life
from his aching lungs.
His breath surrenders.

Catch *your* breath
here.
For you must go on
in his name.

Reading between the lines

I turned to Scripture to sort out my strong reaction to Gibson's film and think through the ways in which this crucial scene could be portrayed. I remembered that nails had been the symbolic focus of the scene in previous years, but the film's sights and sounds still ripped at my memory. Was there not another way to face the cross?

My return visit to the scriptural accounts of the crucifixion surprised me. No Gospel mentions nails. In fact, the only reference to the wounds in Jesus' hands and feet comes in the stories of his resurrection appearance to Thomas. The Bible communicates in a minimalist style. "And they crucified him," says Mark. "There with the criminals," adds Luke. It is a stark and simple statement. I recalled learning somewhere else that death in crucifixion came not from being nailed to a cross, but through suffocation as the body's weight bore down on a frame no longer able to support itself. In this image of Jesus' body bearing the weight of the world, in his surrendering of his breath, I found my in*spiration* for the scene.

The poem grew around the theme "What takes his breath away?" I settled for three themes: pain, fear and tears. Each in its own way can make us draw a sudden breath or breathe raggedly. Each in its own way nailed Jesus to his cross for our sakes. The poem was read very slowly while the heavy cross that had been carried from the village was supported in the crossing of the church. The crowd stood silently, watching. As each theme was named, a black ribbon was bound to the cross – one at each end of the crossbar, and one where we might imagine Jesus' feet would hang. Nails of a different sort, bonds of the humanity Jesus shared with us, bonds of the love that took him to the Cross.

When the poem touched the theme of love, a white bandage was wrapped around the Cross at its centre point. The woman who bound the four ties to the Cross did it with deliberate tenderness. I found this profoundly moving, a deep contrast to the images from the film. In its simplicity and tenderness, I saw the love of God made flesh in the courage and compassion that took Jesus to the Cross. Such love still takes my breath away. Such love compels me to follow.

To be remembered

One of the remarkable opportunities I had working at the island
centres was to observe how people grew into roles as worship leaders.
At least some of the staff members who join the team each year never
before have had a chance to lead. Creating resources that used a
variety of voices often allowed me to invite new participants to gain
experience. The story of Tabitha, in the Book of Acts 9.36-42, is one
of the appointed lessons for the third Sunday after Easter. As I read it
through, I realized that in 25 years of preaching I had never explored
this episode. It seemed like high time! The sermon that emerged
from my reflections needed other readers to join in a conversation I
imagined. For this occasion, I invited a young woman, a new volunteer
with us, to join a mature man and woman in the roles of Tabitha's
widowed neighbours. The interplay of voices was a subtle reminder
that the widowed wear many different faces in our communities. Both
the novice and the experienced participants read with such affection
that the dialogues created a powerful atmosphere. As you read, let
your imagination colour the voices with the cadences of different
generations.

Imagine the scene.
She opens her eyes.
She stands up, a little unsteady on her feet.
Peter takes her hand, leads her to the stairs.
As they begin to make their way down, they hear voices.
"Stop," she whispers.

Voice One: Look at these wee dresses. She sewed them for my girls
last year. See the embroidery! The girls dance in the street
whenever they put them on.

Voice Two: Look at this shirt. Linen, I think. Even my grandmother
never gave me a linen shirt.

Voice Three: She guessed my size. I wore this to my wedding. Tabitha
came, of course. She gave us a tablecloth, too.

Imagine Tabitha, waiting on the stairs,
overhearing what her friends and neighbours are saying about her

the day she died.

Not to be morbid,

but have you ever wondered what people will say about *you* when you're gone?

Have you ever asked yourself

what you'd like people to remember about your life?

Your achievements?

The stories you like to tell?

The difference you've made to someone?

Voice One: She always remembered my girls' birthdays. Seemed to know when they'd grown too big for their last dress. When my husband died, I didn't know what to do with three daughters. But Tabitha knows…uh…knew. She helped them discover their beauty, even though we are poor.

Voice Two: Oh, yes! She made my son a linen shirt. He wears it with pride though he has only one arm. He still has to beg on the street for a living. But Tabitha gave him respect. What a gift!

Voice Three: Oh, yes! She came to our wedding when others wouldn't, knowing there was a baby on the way. She came to our home and ate at our table. Always left us a gift on her way out the door. Then she sat with me when Samuel got sick, night after night, so I could get a little sleep.

Tabitha was quite a woman, it seems.

She is remembered for her good works, her acts of charity.

She is also remembered as a *disciple* of Jesus,

the only woman in the New Testament called by that term.

Surely there were other women disciples,

but Tabitha is the only one given that specific title.

She must have been quite a woman,

for although this story is told to enhance *Peter's* reputation as a miracle-
worker,
the details focus on Tabitha.
It is a story filled with affection for her
as her friends wash her body and lay it out the day she died.
Then they begin to tell stories, as grieving friends will do.
Her neighbours must show each other the gifts of her generosity.
They must tell the stories that clothe *her*
with the respect she gave *them*.
It would be good to know
that people will remember *us* with such affection
once we're gone.

This is an interesting story to read
in the season after Easter.
Tabitha's story made me wonder how Jesus
wanted to be remembered.
What did he hope his friends would recall
from his life
and from all those encounters recorded in the Gospels?
Surely it wasn't the miracles he wanted us to focus on.
Again and again,
he tried to silence the people he had healed.
He asked them *not* to tell others what he'd done for them.
It is interesting to wonder why.
Perhaps he didn't want us to be trapped
by expectations of the miraculous,
the seemingly impossible.
Perhaps he thought we'd get those stories mixed up
because we couldn't explain them properly.

And surely Jesus wasn't interested in giving quotable quotes
to those who asked him questions.
He tended to answer a question with a question of his own.
Or with one of those amusing, annoying stories

188

that seem to have a thousand meanings,
depending on where we stand and what we see.

It was around a table,
eating with the motley crew of disciples he called friends,
that he asked to be remembered.
When he broke the bread,
when he poured out the wine, he said,
"Do this to remember me."
And so the motley crew of disciples called the church
has broken bread
and poured out wine
to remember Jesus
again and again.

When we break bread and share the cup here,
we remember Jesus, broken on the cross for us –
to set us free from the burdens that break our spirit,
the sorrow, the poverty, the unfairness.
We remember Jesus' lifeblood poured out for us –
to refresh us with forgiveness and hope
when life has been spilled and stained
by our own clumsiness and failure.

He took bread and broke it.
This is my body, broken for you.
Do this to remember me.
But did he mean just to break bread to remember him?
I think Tabitha, the disciple, shows us another angle on our
    remembering.
From the testimony of her friends,
it seems that she broke open her life,
her resources,
to share them with those in need.
She poured out her love,

giving gifts to the neediest people around her.
Clothing them with beauty.
Clothing them with hope.
Clothing them with respect.

Is *this* not how *we* should remember Jesus?
Not simply by sharing bread and wine in his name.
But by breaking open our lives
to welcome those who make other people uncomfortable.
To clothe lives exposed to risk with our generosity and skill.
To give beauty,
hope
and respect
to those who need them.
To those whom the world denies such dignity.
Perhaps it is that simple to be a disciple of Jesus.
Perhaps it is that daring to be a disciple of Jesus.

A sociologist who studies trends in church attendance in Canada told
    this story.
He was visiting a Canadian city for a conference
and got talking to the manager of a local restaurant.
The manager was moaning about the trouble he had
finding staff to wait on tables in the restaurant on Sundays,
especially for the Sunday lunch shift.
My colleague's ears perked up.
Perhaps he had stumbled on the *only* city in Canada
where young people preferred to be in church on Sunday,
rather than working in local restaurants!
So he asked the manager
why he couldn't find staff for Sundays.
"Well," said the manager,
"most of our customers on Sunday
are people who come for lunch right after church.
And you know,

those people never leave very big tips."

My colleague laughed a little
and then he shook his head and asked us:
"Wouldn't it be a better story
if people who go for lunch after church on Sunday
were known for their *generosity*?
If we were known as the *biggest* tippers in town?"

How would Jesus want his disciples to be remembered?
Tabitha shows us
through the miracle of her generosity.
Could we, too, be remembered
for the possibilities we create –
for the hope,
for the beauty,
for the respect we offer to others –
because we care enough to clothe lives in need
with gifts fashioned by our love and concern?

Imagine the scene.
You are coming down the stairs,
unseen by friends who miss your presence:

Voice One: Remember the time she stood up for me when no one else
                believed me....

Voice Two: Remember when he loaned me the money when I couldn't
                even open a bank account...

Voice Three: Remember how she used to come over and help...

Voice One: Remember how he listened when...

Voice Two: Remember...

Voice Three: Remember...

Reading between the lines

The story of Tabitha is one of a series of events that lift up Peter as a leader among the apostles after Jesus' resurrection. His power to heal reflects Jesus' own miracles of healing. This story in Acts has many similarities to Jesus' healing of Jairus' daughter. In that story, too, a plea is sent out and the healer comes to a home struck by tragedy. There, too, Jesus clears the room of onlookers before he "awakens" the young girl. I was attracted by the similarities between the stories at first, but a little research into the details showed that I could not press those similarities too far. The words used in the original stories differ. I decided to pay attention to the *differences* that distinguish Tabitha's story from earlier gospel accounts about Jesus' healings.

I found it an interesting exercise to visualize her story, because there are many more details provided about Tabitha than about the other people Peter healed. Tabitha must have been someone her friends remembered with deep appreciation. Perhaps she was someone of great importance, too. She is called a *disciple*, a word that occurs only this once in the New Testament. It is the female form of the word used to refer to Peter and the other male disciples. Contrary to common opinion, Jesus had at least one woman disciple! Tabitha had a ministry among the widows of her town, sewing for them. Suddenly I was in the room with them, as they gathered to remember her, bringing along samples of her handiwork. I recalled meetings with grieving families when people had to tell certain stories about a precious life that had just ended. They wanted to show me the tokens of that life they could hold on to. Here was the aspect of the story to which we could all relate. Surely we all treasure something left to us by a compassionate friend or neighbour. Surely we all have some tangible token of love whose story we like to tell.

As I went back through the story with this conviction in mind, I was struck by how much more of the story concerned Tabitha herself, not Peter's miracle. I wondered if her story was really placing Tabitha as a leading disciple alongside Peter in the records of her community. The miracle in Tabitha's ministry was not her resurrection. The miracle was her compassion that wrapped those in need with the warmth of her love. It was *this* miracle her friends remembered with each other. By allowing the details of the storytelling to shape my insight into the meaning of the story, I was struck with the privilege of meeting Tabitha through the voices of her friends. I wanted to honour her ministry and its significance to the lives she touched. I realized this is also what I do when retelling a story about Jesus – to honour not only his gift to others but also the very lives he touched. For in their response to Jesus, we are invited to make *our* response. In Tabitha, we see both the example of a disciple responding to Jesus and the impact discipleship can make.

The story about tipping comes from Canadian sociologist Reginald Bibby. He told it at a conference where we were both speaking. It's a good story. I chose to use it near the end of this sermon to relieve any pressure on listeners whose fresh grief might have been stirred up through their own remembering that day. From another angle, the story presents us with the truth we meet in Tabitha. Discipleship is rooted in generosity. The story had the same effect in Iona Abbey that it had when I first heard it. There was knowing laughter followed by some rather uncomfortable silence. Bibby put his finger on an important point. Small acts of generosity and charity are not easy. We ought not to take them for granted. They are the making of disciples. They proclaim Good News.

The unique feature of the story, in my imagining, is that Tabitha might actually overhear her friends talk about the impact she'd had. Wouldn't it be illuminating for any of us to discover what people will honour about us after we've died? With this in mind, I wanted to create strong visual impressions for my listeners so they might put themselves in the scene. Whether they reflected on the legacy of their own lives or remembered the generosity of others, I hoped to connect those memories to Jesus and the impact his disciples can have. The beginning and the ending of the sermon parallel each other, but the ending leaves us held in our own context, looking and listening to lives connected to ours. People listened attentively, in the way we do when a friend recounts a precious memory of someone who has died. There was no doubt that many people were moved to deeper reflection. I can only hope they may be moved to deeper action, too.

When the penny drops

Stories have a remarkable power to draw us into truth we might otherwise avoid. They are also easier for many people to grasp than sustained argument. Stories often help children participate in worship because they can imagine a scene and know how it would feel to be there. No wonder the Gospel comes to us in stories! This reflection was developed for an evening service when a large church youth group were guests at the MacLeod Centre. Working with the story told by Jesus in Luke 15.8-10 and with the episode from David's life found in 2 Samuel 11–12.7, I wove in stories and sayings young people could identify with. The Scripture was read in small portions by voices other than my own, as were the stories from our own times. To give time for reflection, we used the chant "Take, O take me as I am," found in Chapter 1 of this book.

Steven Spielberg, the famous American movie producer,
   knows stories.
His movies are incredibly popular.
A story, said Spielberg,
does not have a beginning, a middle and an end.
A story has a beginning that keeps beginning.
Think about it.
Often when we hear someone tell a story,
it reminds us of something similar that happened to us.
We may not even wait for someone to finish before we burst in,
"That reminds me of the time…."
And so the story keeps beginning.
That's what happened at Bible study when I read this story aloud:

Voice One: What woman having ten silver coins,
              if she loses one of them,
              does not light a lamp, sweep the house,
              and search carefully until she finds it?
              When she has found it,
              she calls together her friends and neighbours, saying,
              "Rejoice with me, for I have found the coin that I lost."

Just so, I tell you,
there is joy in the presence of the angels of God
over one sinner who repents.

A participant raised her hand.

Voice Two: I know what that's like.
When my sister-in-law got engaged to my brother,
they came home to show us her beautiful diamond ring.
That afternoon, we went to the supermarket to shop for
dinner.
When we got home,
the diamond was gone from her ring.
We hunted everywhere.
No diamond.
We went back to the store to explain
that the diamond had to be somewhere in *that* store.
The manager told us to come back at closing time.

As we listened to this new story,
the daunting prospect of searching a giant supermarket seemed
overwhelming.
The story had us hooked.

Voice Two: There we were at midnight,
down on hands and knees in an acre of grocery store.
I thought the diamond was gone for good,
but my sister-in-law wouldn't give up.
Four hours later she found it —
on the floor against some shelves by the soup.
We had the biggest engagement party you can imagine!

As this story unfolded,
I could see curiosity,
then sympathy,
then disbelief

on the faces of those who listened.
We laughed in delight as we pictured a diamond jubilee
at four o'clock in the morning!
Our own surprise and pleasure in this story
became a new parable of God's surprise and pleasure
over the lost coin of a life restored to God's safekeeping.
So God and the angels celebrate
when at last, for us,
the penny drops.
When we have a change of heart
and reach out to receive God's engaging embrace,
the angels will dance for joy
like those diamond-hunters cheering in a deserted food store.
We need this story to keep beginning,
over and over again in our hearts,
so that we trust the promise that God rejoices over us.
Yes, *us*!

Chant

There is another story in Scripture
that has the power to make a penny drop.
It is the story of the prophet Nathan,
who was very unhappy with the behaviour of King David.
The king arranged to claim the wife of one of his soldiers
by sending the soldier into deadly battle.
The soldier died
and David made his move.
Here's what Nathan said:

Voice One: There were two men in a certain city,
                one rich and the other poor.
                The rich man had very many flocks
                but the poor man had nothing but one little lamb,
                which he had bought.

He brought it up and it grew up with him
and his children.
It used to eat of his meagre fare and drink from his cup.
It was like a daughter to him.
Now there came a traveller to the rich man
and he was loath to take one of his own flock
to prepare for the wayfarer.
So he took the poor man's lamb,
and prepared that for the guest who had come to him.

The sad tale of the poor man's lamb gripped David
with its sense of injustice.
This callous rich man took such self-serving advantage
of that poor family's pet.
David was outraged.
"This man has no pity.
He deserves to die!"
But then the penny drops.
Nathan said to David,

Voice One: "You are the man!"

You are the callous rich king
who served your own needs
by claiming Bathsheba and sending Uriah to his death.
The outrage you feel over the lamb
is the very outrage that God feels – over you!

Surely this story lays its finger on our hearts.
We recall times when we have been outraged
by *someone else's* behaviour.
But in any moment of outrage,
we should see our own faces reflected
in the face of King David.
Recall at least one time when you acted

in your own best interest
with no thought for someone else.
Remember one time you didn't keep your promise.
Like David,
we all trip over our own failures,
large or small,
to do justice or show kindness.
So we need this little story
to keep beginning.
It invites us to have a change of heart.
It insists that we face the hurt we've caused
with regret
and with courage that will make peace,
keep a promise
or renew a relationship.

Such stories stir up the stories of our own hearts.
We grasp God's truth
when a penny drops
in our own souls.
When we recognize
that *we* have given offence
by our own actions
just as often as we have taken offence
at someone else's behaviour,
then we know God is waiting to see how we'll respond.

And when our hearts and minds are captured by the truth
that God's forgiveness is for us,
we can hear God's joy.
"Yes!" says that careful housekeeper
as she claims that elusive treasured coin.
"Yes, my beloved! Now I've got you," says our God.
"Grace has claimed you.
And by grace, I will never let you go!"

God treasures all those lives
that are in need of a change of heart.
Like King David's.
Like ours.
Listen to one more parable
written by a member of that study group.

Voice Two: For what woman,
                having dropped a stitch
                while knitting a garment for her beloved,
                will not go back, pick up the stitch
                and rework her whole creation?

Here is a glimpse of God
who works on our lives as patiently
as a grandmother knitting tiny garments for a new baby.
With loving fingers of grace,
God unties the knots of our lives.
God helps to untangle the mistakes we've made.
God smoothes out our twisted stories
and reworks them by the power of the Spirit.
The story of the Good News can begin again for us,
within us,
no matter how old we are,
where we've wandered,
what corner we've taken refuge in.
God rejoices to find our hearts awakened,
our minds opening to a new possibility for ourselves.

Chant

Reading between the lines

In discussions of Celtic spirituality, a question about the place of women was raised from time to time. Some people cherish the hope that Celtic Christian roots offer a source of deeper appreciation for the significance of women as participants in community life and as the female face of the image of God. Certainly, women saints are often numbered among those names called on in prayer and storytelling within Celtic lore. Mary, mother of Jesus, is a constant companion, too. Yet the legends about St. Columba are more complicated with regard to his view of women in community. The Isle of Women, a small island across the sound from Iona just off the coast of Mull, is said to be the place where Columba sent women to stay. Some stories say that female animals were banished to that place, too! The fact that Adomnan had to object to the mistreatment of women and children in the society of his day suggests we should be careful not to expand liturgical references to female saints into an idealized era for the daily lives of women.

As a Christian feminist, I enjoy lifting up for fresh consideration those Scripture texts where women characters play a central role. In my theological training, I was often frustrated by the history of biblical interpretation when male characters were taken to be examples of *human* behaviour and symbols of *God's* nature whereas women in parallel stories were demoted to represent *only* women's lives – and more to the point, women's *failings*. Interpretations of the small parable at the hinge of this service often scolded the woman for losing the coin rather than seeing her joy as God's rejoicing. The shepherd in the parallel parable is never scolded for losing a sheep, but applauded for his diligent search. I decided to use just the parable of the housekeeper to let her face shine before us. Nathan's parable offers the reminder that God not only treasures us, but also calls us to live responsibly with others. When we must face up to harm we have caused – and we must – we can do so remembering that God will rejoice when we make a new beginning.

The stories I retold in the reflection emerged during a women's retreat when we explored a number of Jesus' parables. Parables have a way of turning expectations upside down. Some of the women at the retreat felt defeated by their personal histories. Exploring parables generated confidence and excitement that God's grace really embraced *them*. Their storytelling in response to Scripture naturally drew on experiences from their own lives. This was hardly an occasion of feminist subversion. It was truly a time of rejoicing in God's grace, celebrated in symbols that made sense to those lives. Many young people I meet often struggle to recognize any value in their lives, just as some of those women had. I hoped that the women's stories might offer to my younger listeners a sense that God's grace is for their lives, too.

I was honestly quite surprised by a letter the Warden received a few days after this service. The writer, an older man, took deep exception to my use of female figures, which he found deliberately provocative and offensive. In such response, one feels the impact of traditional interpretations that do not reflect the text of Scripture itself. I was grateful that the Iona Community intends to honour the freedom of both Scripture and preacher to challenge our expectations of what we think we know. This small parable challenges the traditional assertion that because Jesus called God "Father," God must always be spoken of in male terms. In the teaching of Jesus and in the stories of Jesus' relationships with women, there is radical power to redeem lives, to re-establish value and direction in any lives – male or female – that have lost touch with God. I continue to confess my faith in Jesus who offers all of us, whatever our gender or generation, the touch of God's grace and friendship.

6

With Gifts of Courage, Faith and Cheerfulness

Many people find worship at Iona Abbey refreshing. Those who return regularly to one of the island centres look forward to the renewing time spent in worship as well as in walking the hills. When I reflect on my years on Iona, preparing and leading worship was truly the most rewarding of my tasks. Yet this appreciation for worship in the Abbey casts a shadow for many of us. Guests and staff members alike often despair that their home churches will never catch a breath of this fresh air to inspire worship there.

St. Columba has a word for those of us who have been nourished through time spent at the Abbey – and for readers who enjoy exploring creative worship resources in print. Remember that Columba did not cultivate his community on Iona as a place for followers to come and settle. He expected those who studied with him to move on, contributing to other communities of worship, study and witness in places God led them. Columban communities, sprinkled around Britain, held many features of worship in common but none were simply copies of Iona. One scholar of Columba's influence speaks of the "provisional" quality of the monastic life he initiated, proclaiming the presence of God through worship and pastoral life but not setting down institutional practices to be safe-guarded. A frustrating feature for historians of this period is the lack of written sources to establish exactly how Columba and his community prayed. Documents available come from decades or even centuries later! Perhaps the best gift to take away from Iona is a sense of courage and creativity to set our lives before God in worship, being honest about our predicaments, and trusting God to make a real and redeeming difference.

Each Wednesday morning, worship at the Abbey concludes with the words of a prayer that reminds us of Columba's intent. It begins with these words:

> O God, who gave to your servant Columba the gifts of courage, faith and cheerfulness, and sent people from Iona to carry the word of your gospel to every creature: grant, we pray, a like spirit to your church, even at this present time…. (The Iona Abbey Worship Book, p. 20)

This prayer is also found in the Iona Community members' book as a prayer for the whole Community. The renewal of prayer and worship throughout the Church has been a central concern for the Community, reaching back to George MacLeod's original desire for the parish at his doorstep. The Community continues to seek "new ways to touch the hearts of all," as the Wednesday prayer puts it. The work of the Wild Goose Resource Group is known worldwide as one of the Community's sources of inspiration, providing new music and texts for worship that open up the Gospel from fresh angles. At various times each year, the Resource Group and its incredibly talented friends offer opportunities at the island centres to explore new ways to do Bible study and to enrich worship through song and drama. Their work inspired me to seek clarity in both prayer and preaching, to combine honesty and hope in the words I offer.

The more I became aware of who comes to worship in Iona Abbey, the more I tried to offer a variety of approaches to my theme within the same service. A new way to touch one heart does not always reach every heart! This chapter offers four different ways to tell stories, any one of which could be used within the framework of a local liturgy. However and whenever they are told, stories carry a power to engage hearts in unexpected ways. Each of these models of storytelling offers a different way to join in or reflect upon the story – a musical refrain, a spoken response, a tableau with actors speaking, a dialogue using different voices. Given the encouraging response I received to the following resources, I think that many local churches are waiting to be touched in new ways. So often worship planners hold back from adding something a little different to a regular service because we anticipate rejection. In my parish experience, I found that resistance to change within the liturgy usually reflected people's anxiety that they would lose their familiar routes into God's presence. Being able to weave new and familiar elements together in worship for a local church is an important skill for caring and creative leaders to develop.

No one has to travel all the way to Iona to be touched by God in a new way. Any worship service calls us out of the normal patterns of our day to be present in a new way to all that surrounds us. Worship opens our eyes and invites us to look afresh at God's world. Perhaps we could think of liturgy as a map, providing participants with different starting points and routes to guide them toward God. For some people, music leads and opens hearts. This will be their primary route. For others, just a few of the spoken words or a time of gentle silence will prove surprisingly full of God's presence. Whichever part of the route of a service is familiar or easily accessible, participants can claim confidence there to engage what is new or more challenging. Too many steep learning curves in every service will tire out a worshipper, however, just like a long, steep hike taken at too fast a pace. When we plan worship, let us set out complementary routes, any one of which provides important steps on the way, and all of which lead toward God's promises proclaimed that day.

The gates of heaven

This sermon was prepared for Sunday morning during a week led by the Wild Goose Resource Group. The theme for the week was "Heaven on Earth," considering unusual angles on familiar stories from Jesus' ministry. When I consulted the lectionary for that Sunday, the story in Genesis 28.10-17 caught my fancy. Jacob's vision of angels descending from heaven to earth seemed so apt for our theme, even though it wasn't a story about Jesus. As you read what follows, you will keep encountering a refrain from a song by John Bell and Graham Maule, "The God of Heaven Is Present on Earth", found in *One Is the Body* (© Wild Goose Resource Group, 2002). The congregation sang this refrain as I moved from one part of the Abbey to another, something I don't usually do during a sermon. As I explain later, I had an instinct about how this ancient story and the ancient site of the Abbey could work together. As you read what follows, let yourself pause over each chorus to think about the story that has just been told and the affirmation of faith the song proclaims.

This is none other than the house of God.
This is the gate of heaven.

Jacob was running away from trouble.

He had cheated his brother.

He'd lied to his father.

He and his mother disguised the truth to save his sorry skin.

Jacob headed out of town to get away before his brother Esau could kill him.

He came to a certain place, so the story goes.

No place in particular.

He stopped because the sun had set.

Taking one of the stones of the place as a pillow,

he laid his sorry skin down to sleep.

Not exactly the setting for a good night's sleep.

Was he troubled by what he'd done?

Was he afraid of what the future held?

In such a state, I might have lain awake all night, sorting and scheming.

But Jacob, schemer that he was,
suddenly discovered himself at the gate of heaven.

In a scene reminiscent of the Moulin Rouge,
God's angels rustled their way up and down a stairway from heaven.
In his dreams, God had Jacob's attention.
And God promised that Jacob would receive a blessing,
even though he was running away from everyone he knew
– and everything he'd done.
Jacob was no angel.
Yet God was faithful to him
when his future was in doubt.
Jacob awakened, stunned by his vision and a little afraid of its
    implications.
"Surely the Lord is in this place
And I did not know it."

> *This is none other than the house of God.*
> *This is the gate of heaven.*

Do you recognize Jacob's astonishment?
Have you ever found yourself standing at the gate of heaven
when you least expected it?
When the future was in doubt?

Refrain

THE GOD OF HEAVEN IS PRE - SENT ON EARTH IN

WORD AND SI - LENCE AND SHA - RING, IN FACE OF DOUBT, IN

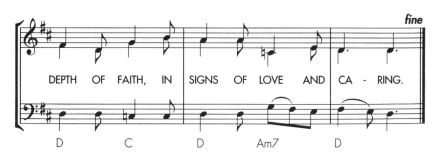

DEPTH OF FAITH, IN SIGNS OF LOVE AND CA - RING.

I had to stand on tiptoe to see through the porthole in the door.

Inside, lights were bright.

Nurses were busy, crouched over the bubbles that contained fragile
    newborns.

I was ushered to an incubator in the middle of the room.

"Here he is."

I had never seen such a tiny baby.

Born more than two months premature, he had little hope of seeing
    the morning.

His mother wanted him baptized.
For a moment I could only stare at this wee boy,
smaller than the doll I had rocked when I was a child.
I carried a tiny vial of sterile water.
"By what name is this child known?"
His father swallowed hard.
"Edward," said his mother with more confidence than I could
    muster.
Three drops of water on my finger;
three gentle marks on his tiny forehead.
His mother smiled through her tears as we left,
trusting that God cradled Edward's fragile life.

> *This is none other than the house of God.*
> *This is the gate of heaven.*

Edward surprised the doctors who had turned off his life support.
He lived four months.
He was cuddled and fed his mother's milk with an eyedropper.
His parents read him *Winnie the Pooh*.
He even left that sterile bubble and came home for a few weeks.
He died in his mother's arms.
She said to me, "I wanted Edward to be baptised
not because I thought God would love him more.
I wanted to tell the world that even with all the things that went wrong
    for him,
Edward was a *person* God loved."

Refrain

"Stop here."
The jeep pulled to the side of the road.
We unlocked our doors and looked around cautiously.
You don't ride in a car in Guatemala unless the doors are locked.
I thought I was looking at a cornfield ready for harvest.

A beautiful volcano loomed on the horizon.

Martina led us through the grain.

We came to a white wooden cross planted in the field, partly hidden by the corn.

Suddenly I realized what had happened in that place.

The name on the cross was Manuel, her husband.

He had been murdered in that cornfield a year earlier.

He was a pastor.

He documented human rights violations in his parish.

One night he didn't come home.

A cross marked the place where he died.

As I looked into Martina's eyes, I saw the pain and the courage of his memory.

She had moved house six times in the intervening year.

She, too, was a target.

She wanted me to see that place.

Holy ground.

The gate of heaven.

Refrain

Easter 1979.

My first Easter in my first parish.

Newly ordained, I admit I was a girl minister,

so young I often blazed in where wiser angels feared to tread.

My parish was filled with Canadians of Highland Scots descent,

most of whom were old enough to be my grandparents.

We are part of a Church that celebrates communion infrequently.

Four times a year is supposed to be enough.

I asked the elders when we should plan those four precious times.

They had no idea.

They had not had their own minister for years.

In my youthful cunning,

I proposed we mark every major Christian season or festival with communion.

Advent, Christmas, Epiphany, Lent,
Easter, Pentecost, World Communion.
Somehow they failed to notice we had zoomed from four to seven!
Oh so clever.

Easter Day dawned.
None of us had celebrated Easter with communion before.
We were unprepared for the wonder.
Now, Presbyterians approach the communion table with penitent
    hearts,
remembering we have fallen short of the glory of God.
But we are not used to glimpsing that glory.

If angels descended upon Jacob unawares,
then so did the risen Christ descend that day
on that unsuspecting congregation and its minister.
As we sang the great hymns of resurrection,
as the bread was broken,
eyes were opened
and we recognized him.

> *This is none other than the house of God.*
> *This is the gate of heaven.*

After the service
one of the elders came to me,
Alex, a short, wiry man,
a farmer well past 70.
These days he said little,
except to comment on the odds in an upcoming horse race.
Alex looked at me with tears in his eyes.
"In all my life, I never knew it could be like this."

> *Surely the Lord is in this place*
> *And I did not know it.*

Neither did I, Alex. Neither did I.

Refrain

Jacob's dream of heaven on earth
is for people like me and Alex.
One of us a bit cunning.
One of us a bit world weary.
Neither of us expecting to meet God in our very midst.

Jacob's dream of heaven on earth
is for Martina
and for her neighbours:
some days, filled with sorrow and fear;
other days, filled with anger and courage.
God's promise does not desert us
though the world turns against us.
God speaks through blood shed
in a cornfield
and on a cross.
God promises to suffer with us
until a new day breaks.

Jacob's dream of heaven on earth
is for Edward
and his parents
in their insistence that every moment counts,
that every life counts.
God's promised future embraces every life,
whether brief or ambitious,
whether successful or sorrowful.
God's promise
is delivered by angels
like Edward
and Martina

and Alex
and all those whose lives remind us
that we are never too young
or too poor
or too old
or too ill
or too dangerous
or too used up
for God to say something *to* us.
And
for God to say something *through* us.

Refrain

Reading between the lines

When I begin a sermon on a familiar Bible story, I do what is called a close reading of the Scripture in English translation. I am looking and listening for words and phrases that catch my attention. I often read a familiar story out loud and let the language dance on my lips. This time, the phrase "a certain place" caught me. If a word or phrase hooks me, I study it with all the support I can find – dictionaries, commentaries on the original language, other translations and interpretations. This time, a paradox struck me – in an uncertain time and in a place of no particular importance, Jacob encountered heaven on earth. So often people look for God in special places – a holy island such as Iona or a holy building such as Iona Abbey. But this time, Jacob met God in a rather obscure place when he wasn't in a particularly holy frame of mind.

Provoked by this thought, I began to recall times in my ministry when I had experienced surprising encounters with God. I thought about people I'd met along the way who had reached out to God in times of personal upheaval and uncertainty. I began to recognize many places where I'd been challenged by God, places where I had in fact been *un*prepared to encounter God's presence. The stories I chose to tell in this sermon happened at different points over nearly 20 years. I've changed a few details to protect the identity of my companions. Even after all this time, however, I still felt deeply moved and honoured by what these wonderful people shared with me. I thought that their stories might touch others who were facing times of deep struggle with the hope that God can still surprise us in uncertain times and unexpected places. I tried to tell the stories very simply, with as few details as possible. There is no need in public worship to offer the most unsettling details of a story, especially when it involves suffering. I tried to be fair to both the struggle and the faithfulness of these people, knowing that I had been changed by the way they spoke of God to me.

As I worked on the sermon, I decided that the theme of encountering heaven on earth in unexpected places could shape the delivery of the sermon, too. Iona Abbey is peculiar in its architecture, asymmetrical and a bit awkward in shape as cathedrals go. Wherever you sit or stand, you can see or be seen by only part of the congregation. Jacob's story challenged me to claim the whole Abbey while I preached, to witness to the truth that any place could be a gate of heaven. I chose to tell each story at a different place in the Abbey, drawing the attention of the congregation to an unusual place. In order to create time for movement and for reflection, I inserted the chorus of the wonderful "Heaven on earth" song at key points.

Edward's story took me from the leader's desk, where I began the sermon, back toward the entrance to the church, where I stood facing the baptismal font. For Martina's story, I came to the "crossing," the open heart of the church where the "arms" of the building reach out to suggest the shape of a cross. I told Alex's story standing in front of the communion table where we would celebrate communion later that morning. I returned to the leader's desk to conclude.

I wondered how listeners would respond. Preachers in the Abbey do not often move about while they preach. I know that unexpected movement by someone leading worship can put listeners on edge or draw unnecessary attention to oneself. But in this case, I believe the whole Abbey was proclaiming the promise of the text. Many listeners were deeply engaged, leaning forward, watching, waiting. I felt more fully connected to every listener. The times of singing, when I walked slowly to the next point, allowed the power of the stories to settle and gave people a way to release their own responses through the song. This helped move people through the drama of the stories, rather than letting tragic aspects become overwhelming. I can honestly say that in all my years preaching, I have never had so much response to a sermon. Throughout the following week, many people wanted to talk about what the stories drew out of them and about the topography of preaching. What seemed to me like a risk was received as a gift. God, indeed, is full of surprises.

The stones cry out

The opening responses for Morning Prayer at Iona Abbey rehearse this couplet each day:

Leader: If Christ's disciples keep silent
All: these stones would shout aloud. (Luke 19.40)

As we say these lines together, we are surrounded by the ancient stones that make up the Abbey walls. Many of them have the pink tones of granite, cut elsewhere and hauled to Iona across the water to take their place amid other stone-faced disciples. These rocks have witnessed hundreds of years of worship on this holy ground. As different from each other as the worshippers who gather in their embrace, the stones testify to God's creativity and enduring presence in various ways and varying lives. The stones shouted a welcome over the years when the Abbey lay in ruins, when the groups of worshippers who gathered there to sing and pray had no roof to shelter them. The stones echo now with the music of daily worship, the storytelling of Abbey tour guides and the footfalls of those who keep late-night vigils. I brought this story to Iona Abbey from another place and another time because Luke's story (19.36-40) is so prominent in our daily worship.

(Listeners take the part of the pebbles in this story. At each point where the text is in bold type, the storyteller encourages everyone listening to call out "Hosanna!")

Imagine what it's like to be a rock, a small hard round stone, lying in the middle of a dirt road. When people travel, they kick dust in the face of a rock. When carts carry grain to market, they roll on top of the rocks and stones without blinking.

Micah ben Feldspar was such a rock who lived on the road just outside Jerusalem.

"People walk all over us," he complained to the pebbles lying beside him. "This place would be dust – or mud – without us! But folks just kick us out of the way, as if we didn't matter."

"I know," said Sandy Stone, who landed beside Micah one day. "Maybe these people can't hear us when we talk to them."

"Or else they just don't pay attention to rocks and stones," Micah grumbled.

As the sun rose and the day got hotter, the rocks could feel a distant rumbling in the ground. "What's going on?" the stones and pebbles asked each other.

"It feels like a parade is coming," said Sandy.

"Or a caravan of camels," Micah shuddered.

The pebbles began to jiggle with excitement. "Here they come!" The rocks could see dust rising.

"It is a parade," said Sandy. "Look! The people are waving palm branches."

"Listen to them sing and cheer," Micah said.

Not far off they could hear people singing and shouting, "Hosanna! Hosanna!"

Sandy called out, "I can see someone on a donkey. People are cheering for him!"

"Watch out!" cried Micah. Then he coughed as a palm branch landed right on top of him.

"Join in!" Sandy urged. "It must be the king. Hosanna!" she sang.

And the pebbles replied, "Hosanna! Hosanna!"

"Hosanna," grumbled Micah, who was still underneath a palm branch. The parade walked right over top of him.

The little donkey carrying the king stepped carefully over the singing rocks. Along the road, Micah peeked out from under his branch. "Look at his face," he said in wonder.

"I think he looks very kind," said Sandy. "I bet that he can hear the voices of the stones."

So the pebbles cried even louder, "Hosanna! Hosanna!"

As all the stones and pebbles watched the parade go by, they heard some angry men try to stop the singing.

"Teacher!" the men shouted, "Silence your disciples!"

The king said, "I tell you, if these were silent, the very stones would cry out."

"He did hear us. He heard our song!" shouted Micah.

The pebbles sang again, "Hosanna! Hosanna!"

When the parade was over, and the next day arrived, life returned to normal for the rocks on the road. People coming to Jerusalem walked on top of them. Children picked them up and tossed them at walls, or at soldiers who weren't watching. It was a busy road and those rocks had a busy life, keeping the dust down.

But on Friday, things changed.

The earth began to rumble again.

A troop of Roman soldiers marched out early that morning, their boots crunching hard on the rocks in the road.

"Ouch! Ouch!" cried the stones and the pebbles. "Your boots hurt!"

Along came another crowd.

"Is this a parade, too?" wondered Sandy Stone.

"No! Listen," whispered Micah. "Their voices are angry."

Then the rocks felt tired footsteps dragging something heavy through the dust.

"Look!" said Sandy softly. "It's the king."

"But he's bleeding," said Micah. "Stop! Listen to us!" Micah cried louder. "You are hurting the king!"

All the pebbles called, "Hosanna! Hosanna!"

"No one is listening to us," Sandy sighed.

"They are going to kill the king," frowned Micah.

The pebbles wept sadly, "Hosanna! Hosanna!"

All at once the sky turned black and the ground trembled. The rocks were afraid and the pebbles were silent.

Then Sandy cried out, "No! Keep singing. Keep singing for the king!"

So one by one,
the rocks
and the stones
and the pebbles joined in. "Hosanna! Hosanna!"

"Louder!" called Micah.

"Hosanna! Hosanna!" they shouted together.

"HOSANNA! HOSANNA!"

Nothing would keep the rocks from singing their song for the king.

So let nothing keep us from singing our song in praise of the King, Jesus.

Hosanna! Hosanna!

Reading between the lines

This story was originally written for children joining in a community service on Palm Sunday evening. The preacher on that occasion had chosen "The stones cry out" from Luke 19 as his text. I wanted to tell this familiar story from an angle a child could identify with. Children are so often smaller than their surroundings, looking up at a world designed by and for adults. They are often overlooked, talked over, ignored. As I imagined the scene on the road into Jerusalem, I thought that the stones sat in a place common to many children. Jesus' words of challenge in Luke's story suggested that he might be as alert to the presence of stones, as sensitive to *their* voices, as he had been to the children around him. So I wrote the story as if I were a stone, lying on the road looking up at the events of Palm Sunday happening over top of me. Whenever I tell it, I always invite the children who listen to take the part of the pebbles and join in the cry Hosanna! Hosanna!

The story has been told in many places in Canada. A colleague turned it into a drama for adults and children to act out in worship. Children have sent me copies illustrated with their own drawings. It is a story that draws in its listeners. Wherever I've told it, there is a point when the mood of the listeners becomes very intense, children and adults together. Used on Palm Sunday, it has the impact of pressing us into the drama of Holy Week. The easy cheers that greeted Jesus on his arrival into Jerusalem will turn to the betraying cry "Crucify!" in a few short days. The story prepares our hearts for the deepening drama of Good Friday.

On Iona, during our program called "Experiencing Easter," we used the story in a dramatic form with children taking part according to their age and ability. It was staged not in the abbey, but as one station in our procession that accompanied the cross through the village on Good Friday morning. The youngest children sat on an old stone fence and played the part of the pebbles, jiggling, cheering, whispering, then crying out in fierce determination. Older children played the more demanding roles with all the concentration of those given a serious responsibility. One of the older boys played the role of Jesus, carrying a small cross past the young pebbles toward the end of the story. Then, at the appropriate moment while the pebbles were shouting, an adult shouldering the heavy cross in our procession began to move across the scene, weighed down by his burden. The intensity of the children's cry, "Hosanna! Hosanna!" proved quite stirring to many listeners at that moment. And so it became a memorable story for people in a very different place and time than I had first imagined. But then that is the power of Jesus' story, to move hearts and change lives wherever his story is told.

A beautiful thing

Iona Abbey is a beautiful place in which to worship. Sound and symbol, colour and movement in our liturgies are supported by the lines of the building itself and the flickering candles that encourage those who gather to savour God's beauty and wonder. The story of the woman who anoints Jesus, told in Mark 14.3-9, raises interesting questions about beauty. Jesus' affirmation of her beautiful act pushes us to look more deeply at the place of beauty in our lives and in our relationship with God. The text challenged me to create a liturgy in which we could experience beauty as God's gift. The beauty in this service was conveyed by simplicity of action and word, by sight and sound that all could share. As you read the reflection, imagine a tableau of characters taking their places. A woman of quiet beauty approaches Jesus. Oil glistens in candlelight. A chant from Taizé flows around us to enhance the action of anointing. The rich harmonies in the chant thicken the air like perfume. As with any music from Taizé, this chant allowed us to slow our rhythms for reflection and to breathe in the beauty that embraced us.

Three figures took part in this script alongside a reader and the celebrant. The first figure, a man, entered the Abbey and stood at a microphone a short distance from the communion table set in the centre aisle. He begins the drama:

Simon speaks:
It's funny.
In tonight's story, you'll hear my name but you won't meet me.
I just want you to know I was there.
It happened at my house, after all.
I invited him to supper.
And he came.
His friends weren't too happy to give me the kiss of peace.
But he did.
He was like that…

(short pause)
Ah, my story, I was forgetting.
Well, truly I was remembering.
It's hard to forget that night.

We were sitting around a table, enjoying a meal,
but the night was heavy on our shoulders.
Lots of talk.
Not too much laughter.
Something was bound to happen.
You could smell it in the air.

> *While the reader speaks, Jesus takes his place*
> *at the end of the table.*
> *The woman enters behind him and pours oil on*
> *his head, as the reading continues.*

Reader:
While Jesus was at Bethany in the house of Simon the leper,
as he sat at table,
a woman came with an alabaster jar of very costly ointment.
Nard, it was.
She broke open the jar and poured the ointment on his head.

Chant: *Ubi caritas et amor, Deus ibi est.*
            (Wherever there is charity and love, there is God.)

The woman speaks:
He touched my life with his words.
He answered my questions.
He called me Daughter.
He called me Friend.
He set me free from pain.
He lifted my spirit.
He gave me respect when others judged me.
He saw the beauty in my life when I couldn't.
He blessed my soul.

That night the air was heavy on our shoulders.
I felt somehow I had to show the world the beauty of his life,
the power of his love.

I had to do something
to tell the world how much he meant to me,
to us.
God's anointed one.
The one who poured out so much love and forgiveness
into every life he touched.
I did what I could.
I offered what I had.
And you know what happened.

Reader:
Some there said to one another in anger,
"Why was the ointment wasted in this way?
This ointment could have been sold for more than a year's wages,
and the money given to the poor."
And they scolded the woman.

Chant: Ubi caritas et amor, Deus ibi est.

Jesus speaks:
Let her alone.
Why do you trouble her?
She has done a beautiful thing for me.
You always have the poor with you,
and you can show kindness to them whenever you wish.
But you will not always have me.
She has done what she could;
she has anointed my body beforehand for its burial.
Truly, I tell you,
wherever the Good News is proclaimed in the whole world,
what she did will be told in memory of her.

Chant: Ubi caritas et amor, Deus ibi est.

Celebrant:
Was it the extravagance of her act they didn't like?

Or was it the beauty that bothered his friends?
I wonder.
Each morning in our prayers in Iona Abbey we say the line
"We will not offer to God
offerings that cost us nothing."
These words might remind us of the money we share
for God's purposes in the world.
We could tally up the time we spend in prayer
and in action for others in need.
Such commitments are very important,
as Jesus said.
And it is always possible to do something,
to give something of ourselves,
because there are always people in deep need around us,
whoever we are, and
wherever we find ourselves,
as Jesus said.

What intrigues me, though, is the *beauty* of her act.
That's how Jesus names it.
"She has done a beautiful thing for me."
Did you ever consider doing a beautiful thing for God?
Who, me?
Do a beautiful thing?
Not me!
Perhaps beauty sounds too frivolous?
Perhaps you don't recognize beauty in your life?
Many of us resist beauty –
we're self-conscious about how we look,
how we move in front of others.
We think we can't sing well enough.
We're nervous to show what we've made ourselves.
We're embarrassed to say something beautiful
or to receive someone's compliment

for what they've found beautiful, valuable in us.
In Jesus,
God invites us to recognize the beauty in human life,
in our own lives.

We don't know which woman anointed Jesus that night.
Was she a woman he had healed and restored to dignity?
Was she a woman he talked with, whose insight he affirmed?
Was she a woman with a reputation whom he set free to make a new
    start?
Was she someone who looked after him,
someone who loved him?
Whoever she was,
she had touched the beauty in her life,
the beauty Jesus could see.
And somehow she sensed that the world was about to snuff out
the beauty and grace he offered.
So she dared to pour out her love
as Jesus was to pour out his.

Her offering was beautiful;
it was tender, sensual.
It smelled good
and it could not be hidden.
She took a risk and was condemned by others.
She took a risk and was upheld by Jesus' love.
He said she would be remembered.
So we sit at this table tonight
and remember her love,
offered to proclaim Jesus' love to the world.
May those who sit at other tables with us
recognize the beauty and value in our lives
as we proclaim Jesus' love in what we do and who we are.

Chant: Ubi caritas et amor, Deus ibi est.

The celebration of communion continues.

The Invitation:

We gather at this table
to remember how much God loves us,
and to remember how much love costs.
Come and touch the gifts of God's love for you:
love as fresh as home-baked bread,
love as lively as wine on the tongue.
Come and taste the goodness of God:
broken open,
poured out for you
in Jesus' life with us.
Come and share the goodness of God:
passed from hand to hand,
passed from life to life
in Jesus' name.
Come and know
that all this is for you –
whoever you are,
whatever you've done,
wherever you've been,
however you come.
All this is for you
when you receive these gifts in hopeful expectation.

Reading between the lines

The theme of beauty truly makes some people nervous! When I was
a theological professor, I once taught a course that explored a feminist
author's view of gifts women bring to the ministry of the Church.
Beauty was one of the gifts she named. Almost all my students firmly

rejected that notion. Some argued that women are turned into objects when beauty is emphasized. Others said that notions of beauty are always culturally determined and commercially exploited. Some felt there was no connection between God and beauty. Still others felt judged by the word because they saw no beauty in themselves. The discussion left me feeling sad. While I agreed that beauty can be exploited and objectified, I still hoped my students could recognize the beauty God creates in us and for us, a deeper, purer sense of beauty that will judge the world's concern for fashion. The story of the woman anointing Jesus triggers the same outcry I encountered in class.

Mark's telling of this story highlights Jesus' insistence that this woman's gift of beauty will be remembered. Sadly, Mark didn't think to recall her name. Ironically, Simon the leper *is* remembered by name – himself a silent foil for her beautiful act. Leprosy has such disfiguring effects. But Jesus did not hesitate to enter the home of such a person. He wasn't put off by scars on the surface of a life. As I wondered about the nameless woman and who she might have been, I thought of all the women who had reached out to Jesus. So many of them bore scars of disease or reputation. I decided not to choose any single identity for this woman but to let her stand in for any woman who cannot recognize beauty in herself, anyone whom the world has judged ugly or unworthy. There is beauty in such women and men, though so often they cannot – *we* cannot – see it for ourselves. The condemnation of others restricts our vision. I wanted to lift up Jesus' appreciation for beauty – and his ability to find it in us all.

The theme "In memory of her," set in the context of a meal in a home, readily calls to mind the celebration of communion. The Iona tradition of setting a table down the aisle of the Abbey allowed us to explore many layers in this story. We created a tableau with three figures: Simon, the woman, and Jesus at one end of the table. The woman anointed Jesus in a simple, silent action that made us aware of its tender beauty as we watched. Then a reader who was out of sight interrupted with the objections, reading from the biblical story.

As celebrant for the evening, I sat at the other end of the table from these figures. I can only say it gave me a powerful sense of Jesus in our midst as we broke the bread and poured out the cup that evening. Not that the man who had taken Jesus' role made anything more of himself than the biblical words he read from the story allowed. But somehow having symbolized the scene while we were all at the same table drew us into the beauty of the moment and its promise for us all. In the Reformed tradition, we always begin our celebration of the Sacrament with an invitation to the table. This invitation was created to complete the reflection on the biblical drama we had entered into. It reiterates the possibility that there is beauty in all of us, whether or not we can see it in ourselves. Touching the beauty God creates through us and for us was the gift we received that night.

Give them something

On Sunday mornings in Iona Abbey, the worship service includes a sermon and the celebration of Holy Communion. It lasts more than an hour. The liturgy is printed in *The Iona Abbey Worship Book* so all can join in the spoken and sung responses. There are bibles to follow along with the morning reading, and likely one or two song books to consult. All of this can make worship rather daunting for children, especially when they come to the Abbey for the first time. I wrote this sermon at a point when I knew there were quite a few children among our guests. Just in case those children had to struggle to follow what was happening in all those books, I wanted to be sure they could follow the sermon! The Scripture text assigned for the Sunday was the story of the miracle known as the feeding of the five thousand, found in Mark 6.30-38. A good choice for children and for adults. Miracle stories puzzle all of us!

The disciples had been busy.
Jesus sent them off two by two into the surrounding villages
to heal the sick
and talk about the kingdom of God.
He told them to carry nothing with them.
They had to count on the hospitality of strangers for *every* meal
and a bed at night.
Now I don't know about you,
but I'd find that kind of journey pretty scary.
I wouldn't know just where to start or what to say.
I'd be a little anxious inviting myself to dinner every night.
I might even tuck some money in my shoe just in case.

But good things happened.
Sick people were healed.
Anxious people found peace.
God's good news spread.
The disciples came back with stories to tell Jesus.

Voice One: "It worked, just like you said."
Voice Two: "She took my hand and walked, just like that."

230

Voice One: "You should have seen his face.
              The pain fell away from his eyes as I watched."

I imagine Jesus smiled as they talked.
They were amazed by what happened.
Healing gifts came from ordinary hands.
Peace spoken in ordinary words changed lives.
His friends were excited and exhausted by their adventure.
They needed some rest.
And they needed to think about what had happened.

But life with Jesus in those days sounds a little bit like a weekend on
    Iona –
when a cruise ship sends out its visitors
just as another bus trip arrives.

Voice One: "Many were coming and going,
              and they had no leisure even to eat."

So Jesus said to his friends:

Voice Two: "Come away to a deserted place and rest awhile."

They headed out for a sail and a little peace and quiet.
But someone saw them leave and guessed where they were going.
So another crowd was waiting on the shore
when they got to that *deserted* place.

I imagine the disciples were disappointed.
They were looking forward to a little quiet time with Jesus.
They had stories to tell him.
They wanted him to know just what they'd done
for him.
But there was *another* crowd.
And Jesus plunged into its midst.

Voice One: "There he goes, telling another one of his stories."

Voice Two: "We won't see him till dinnertime."

Voice One: "Dinnertime! Who will make dinner for this crowd?"

Voice Two: "Maybe we can send them back to the mainland to buy a proper meal."

But Jesus wouldn't turn his back on that flock.

He had something they wanted.

God's Word.

God's love.

The bread of life.

No matter how tired he was that day,

no matter how many times he'd faced a big crowd,

no matter how much he wanted a quiet moment with his friends,

he couldn't turn his back on people who needed what he had to share.

Then it got late.

The disciples heard their stomachs rumbling.

So they caught Jesus' attention.

Voice One: "It's nearly dinnertime."

Voice Two: "This is a deserted place."

Voice One: "People are hungry."

Voice Two: "Send them to buy dinner before it gets too late."

I imagine Jesus smiled.

I expect he chuckled or sighed to himself.

His friends hadn't really understood their adventure.

Voice One: "You give them something to eat."

Say what, Jesus?

You've got to be joking.

Feed this crowd?

With what?

Words of goodwill?

Grass for the sheep?
Finally one of them spoke up:

Voice Two: "Jesus?"

Voice One: "Yes, Peter."

Voice Two: "It would take a year's wage to buy dinner for this lot.
Are we supposed to spend *our* money and buy food for
them?"

Voice One: "Did I say that, Peter?"

Voice Two: "No. But what else can we do, way out here, miles from
nowhere?"

Voice One: "Share what you have, Peter.
That's all I ever ask.
Share what you have."

If we read a little further in this story,
we'll come across Jesus' best-loved miracle.
Five thousand men were fed that day, says Mark.
Not counting the women and children, says Matthew.
The grumbling disciples turned up five loaves and two fish between
them
and a hungry crowd was fed.
How it happened I don't know.
Some folk emphasize the mysterious, miraculous multiplying of the
loaves.
Others think the disciples' example of sharing
stirred everybody to share what they carried with them that day
so there was enough to go around.
How the crowd was fed doesn't really matter to me.
The real miracle began earlier in the story –
earlier in the week –
when the disciples took a risk and touched lives in pain.

They took a risk and depended on the hospitality of strangers.
And so it was that all kinds of people,
friends and foreigners,
neighbours in need,
discovered they each had something to give each other.
And their gifts made a difference.
Their gifts changed lives.

But the disciples soon forgot that everyone has something to share.
Faced by a hungry crowd a long way from town,
they wanted to pass the problem of feeding them onto somebody
    else.
You don't expect us to help these hungry people, Jesus?
It's not our problem.
Not my department!

But Jesus said,
"You give them something to eat."
He invited the disciples to remember what they'd just learned.
That God's power works through them.
That they *all* had gifts to share –
if only they'd take a look.
If only they'd take a risk.

You see, the biblical word we translate in English as "miracle"
grows from a root word that means "possibility."
Jesus invites his followers to discover what God makes possible
when *we* love our neighbours;
when we *respond* to the people whose lives touch ours.
Amazing, "miraculous" things happen when we take a risk
and help a stranger;
when we remember what *we* have on hand to share with hungry
    people.

A miracle is what God makes possible
through us, for us and among us
by the mysterious power of love.
Jesus is the mysterious power of love,
living a human life,
sighing a human sigh,
rolling his eyes when friends missed the point,
taking a deep breath
and showing them once again
what love makes possible.

There are still hungry people in the world,
crowds of them;
some in African countries where drought defeats the land;
some in our cities and towns
where some people can't earn enough money to feed their kids or
    themselves.
But we are told again and again
there *is* enough food in the world to feed all of us.
Right now.
If we share what we have.

What will love make possible among us
when we consider how to share the fruit of the earth
through agriculture that takes good care of the land
and fair trade that pays people a fair wage for their hard work?
Do we believe that *we* have something to share?
That we *can* make a difference
by what we eat and how we shop and with whom we share?
Jesus believes that.
We can make a difference.

So Jesus says to us:

Voice One: You give them something to eat.

He invites us to remember
that God's power works through us in amazing, miraculous ways.
We *can* give the hungry people in the world good things to eat
because we all have gifts to share.
Love makes it possible to feed the hungry
and heal aching and anxious hearts
when we take a risk
and share ourselves with others.
We can take that risk *any day*
when we remember that's all Jesus asks.
That we share what we have.
When we do,
love will bless us
and make it possible for all the hungry to be fed.
When we share what we have.

Reading between the lines

Miracle stories fascinate many children, even though they become deeply puzzled about *how* things happened. Some adults, too, find miracle stories hard to fit into their understanding of the world, faced with scientific explanations for so many things. Because these ancient stories defy common-sense explanation, many people feel compelled to choose between interpreting them as factual accounts or shrugging them off. This particular miracle story cannot be shrugged off because it is told in some fashion in every Gospel. It is filled with powerful symbols for the Christian community – bread for the hungry; food in the wilderness; abundance for all. I wanted to claim these symbols in a way that would honour the story and also honour my listeners' questions. One way to touch the hearts of all is to respect good questions!

As I studied all of chapter six in Mark's Gospel for this sermon, I became fascinated with the connection between the miracle of feeding and the earlier story, when Jesus sent the disciples out with authority to teach and heal. It seemed to me the disciples' experience of their own power to heal sat at odds with their reaction to Jesus' instruction to feed the people. Perhaps children could identify with the tension between succeeding at something new but then drawing back from the next challenge, still uncertain. I decided to create a dialogue between the earlier story of success and the disciples' hesitation in the miracle story.

But how much reading can one service contain? How much language spoken by one voice can any listener – especially a young listener – take in? The dialogues in the sermon were written to paraphrase the fuller story in Mark's Gospel in a conversational style. I have learned in writing children's stories that conversation between characters keeps a child's attention. Sentences in conversation are short, often simple. The change in speaker helps the listener follow the ideas. In my comments, I deliberately kept my sentences short. I tried to appeal to things about journeys familiar to all who travel to Iona in the height of summer. I also developed a short Jesus and Peter sketch, an honoured Iona tradition, to give Peter a chance to express a common frustration with miracle texts. What are you really telling us, Jesus? Jesus' line "Share what you have" is a simple restatement of the command in the story, one I thought young people could easily remember.

"Share what you have" is also a way we can put our hands on the miraculous. My interpretation linking "miracle" to "possibility" grows from an insight into the Greek words behind the English text. The word we translate as "miracle" has its roots in the verb "I can" and in nouns that speak of "power" and "possibility." Miracle stories display the power of Jesus in amazing ways. But we, too, can connect with that power when we trust God to make possible through us and for us realities we can never understand or explain. Healing is mysterious. Generosity is also mysterious. These are mysteries in which God is involved, changing the world. We do not always see the results of our prayers or actions in the time frame we might like. But we can act *as if* a miracle is possible, nevertheless. This was the point listeners raised in conversation with me after the sermon. For many, it was a new way to think about how God's power and our own power interact in ways that sometimes amaze us.

The other new aspect for many listeners was the conversation between different voices *within* the sermon. Although I built this in for the sake of children, adults found it refreshing. It helped them pay attention. Preachers saw a new possibility for their own settings. The timing between voices takes a little rehearsal, but it is a very simple way to help listeners of any age follow a sermon. I think it also invites people to be in an inner conversation with the ideas in a sermon, a conversation that may continue beyond the time of worship. This, too, is possible!

7

Pilgrim's Way

Each week, spring through autumn, there is a pilgrimage on Iona led by staff at the island centres. This tradition goes back to the days of George MacLeod who, it is said, led this seven-mile walk in a business suit and street shoes, something to marvel at if you have ever stepped into a bog on Iona! En route, pilgrims stop at points of interest for short reflections and prayers. You may find yourself standing on some of the most ancient rocks at the earth's surface. While I was on staff, the trek was made every week of the season, rain or shine. Often we braved mud, sleet and sunburn to make the journey together, talking, listening, lending a helping hand. The pilgrimage is truly worship with its boots on.

This day-long walk echoes the ancient practice of pilgrimage, an honoured part of Iona's history. Long ago, pilgrims placed themselves in God's hands when they set out, not knowing how their journeys would unfold. To follow a pilgrim's way in those days often meant a way with no return, a way of obedience to God, no matter what the cost. Today, the Iona pilgrimage can be physically demanding, for the path is rough in many places, sometimes steep or slippery. Its challenges give us pause to appreciate the steeper risks undertaken by pilgrims in earlier times. We will find our way back to the Abbey, but we may be changed by the journey. When the Spirit is our companion, there are surprises ahead.

I will never forget the day I led the route with a young couple following close behind me. She was very attentive to him and their conversation seemed quite private. When the day's journey was about halfway through, we sat down beside each other and opened up our lunches. Only then did I realize he was legally blind. She had been describing to him how to approach the next bit of ground every step of the way. He conquered the whole route with a keen spirit of adventure when the wind turned others back. They met the risk and the challenge through great teamwork and good humour. My eyes were opened to what God makes possible when we trust ourselves to walking God's way.

On the Iona pilgrimage, we often climb to a high point where we can see other Hebridean islands – as far as the Isle of Skye, on a clear day. Part of Iona's wonder for me is what lies *beyond* it, when land, sea and sky reveal beauty and mystery yet to be explored. After the pilgrimage, guests in the centres would recognize that their remaining time on Iona was short. They began to talk about going back "into the real world," regretting that time on this holy isle had to end. And yet, wonder still awaits us. We discover truth or insight in spontaneous conversations with people whose paths just happened to cross ours on Iona. Such conversations are cherished gifts. Yet such treasure is to be found in our neighbourhoods, in our workplaces, too, if we take the spirit of adventure, savoured on Iona, into more familiar paths. The reflections in this final section are offered in the spirit of moving on to the place God needs us next.

Living water

One of the stops along the pilgrimage route is Loch Staonaig, in former times the source of drinking water for the island of Iona. Some islanders call it "the Well," I'm told. It is a small loch that glistens in the sunshine on a bright day. Green hills rise around it. For me, it became a good place to catch our breath and wait for slower walkers to catch up. But the loch disguises its deeper reality. If we took a cup of water to refresh ourselves while we sat in the sunshine, we'd find that the water looks like tea. It takes on the brownish tinge of peat in the soil. You'd never guess the colour by looking at the sparkling lake.

The hidden truth of Loch Staonaig reminded me of the hidden truth revealed in the story of the woman at the well in John 4. It seemed like a natural story to tell at this stop on our journey. As you read, imagine yourself standing on the shore of a sparkling lake, a little thirsty at the sight. You have been walking for more than three hours. It is early afternoon. Your feet are a bit tired from some scrambling climbs; your boots a wee bit muddy. You rest your pack on a rocky hillside and the story begins.

They came from different regions.
As different as Scotland and England.
They came from different religions
with the same roots
but different customs.
Different prophets.
Different beliefs.
But they had a common need.
Water.
And they had a common love.
Truth.

"Give me a drink,"
he says.

She looks.
"How is it that you, a Jew, ask a drink from me,
a woman of Samaria?"

He smiles.
"If you knew who was asking,
you would have asked him and he would have given you 'living'
water."

She squints.
"You have no bucket and the well is deep. Where do you get this 'living'
water?"
She challenges.
"Are you greater than Jacob who gave us this well?"

He shrugs.
"If you drink this water, you'll be thirsty again.
The water I will give will become a spring of water, gushing up to
eternal life."

She's no fool.
She's tired of drawing water in the heat of the day.
"Give me this water so I won't have to keep coming to this well."

He points.
"Go, call your husband and come back."

She swallows.
"I have no husband."

He nods.
"You're right. You have had five husbands.
But the man you're living with now is not your husband.
What you have said is true."

She stares.
How could he know that?
"You're a prophet,"
she insists.
"So…tell me who's right? Jews or Samaritans?
We Samaritans worship right here, on this mountain.

You Jews say Jerusalem is the place.
Who is right?"

He stares back.
"God is spirit
and those who worship must worship in spirit and in truth."

She thinks,
What kind of an answer is that?
She declares,
"When the Messiah comes, he will tell us the truth."

He nods.
She has given him her truth.
He offers her his truth.
"I am he.
The Messiah is talking to you."

Hidden truth comes to light when we come face to face with God
and when we come face to face with ourselves.
We need God,
we need truth,
as much as we need water.
In God,
in truth,
we find life.
Sometimes truth, like life, is painful.
But the living water of God's grace cleanses our pain
and renews us to go on.

A prayer:

God,
Reveal to us the truth by which we can live with purpose
and without shame in your world.
Give us courage when we must face painful truth about ourselves.

Make us gentle when we must reveal awkward truth to others.
Cleanse us and renew us by the waters of the earth
and the living water of your love that we taste in friendship and in
faith
day by day.
Amen.

Reading between the lines

Lives, like sparkling water, so often conceal their truth – or at least part of their truth. When I studied the conversation between Jesus and the woman in John's gospel, I was struck to learn that the Greek word for truth, *aletheia*, means "not concealed." When we learn the truth, something hidden is revealed. This Gospel story hints at disguise in its setting. The woman goes to the well in the heat of the day, not the cooler hours when her neighbours most likely filled their water jars. She's a bit suspicious of the stranger who speaks to her. The story leads us further by curious clues. For example, the phrase translated as "living water" can also be read simply as "running water." John loves such mischievous turns of phrase. He offers a skillfully developed drama in which both the woman and the Messiah stand revealed to each other.

When I developed the dialogue, I tried to highlight the puzzles and the clever turns of phrase. Jesus and this woman are sparring with their words. I wanted to present the woman as someone who knows the integrity of her faith, even though many doubt the integrity of her life. When she is put on the spot by Jesus' question, her integrity stands. She acknowledges hidden truth revealed. Here I think she is a parable for us and for all the awkward moments of personal history we'd rather avoid. I believe that only when we acknowledge those moments before God do we discover the deeper truth about God.

From Loch Staonaig, Iona pilgrims continue our journey together with another two hours to go until we reach "home." It was interesting for me to listen to the stories that emerged in those two hours while fellow pilgrims reflected on "truth telling." Somehow the daring character of the woman in this retelling invites listeners to risk a little more of themselves in revealing conversation. In return, the story promises that anyone whose life contains a truth judged unacceptable by others can find release and refreshment face to face with Christ. Told at a point in a day when people have begun to reflect on their faith journeys, the story offered some listeners relief to consider that they didn't have to have done everything right to know that God's truth is for them. In fact, risking our bold questions to God can open up the deeper and surprising truth about our own lives and God's interest in us.

They walked into my life

On Wednesday evening in Iona Abbey, our worship takes the theme of commitment. Often we reflect on what it means for us to be committed to Jesus Christ or to some aspect of his ministry. There is usually a symbolic action during the service, an opportunity for worshippers to move within the church and make a gesture of commitment: for example, to light a candle to show our participation in the Light of Christ. Commitment services are often planned by guests who work with a staff member to choose a theme and weave together words, songs and symbols for our worship.

This monologue was written for a commitment service that I planned with a group of guests during a week led by the Wild Goose Resource Group. The program that week focused on Old Testament passages and their portrayal of God's love and justice. In the spirit of the week, we decided to use a text from the Old Testament to explore God's commitment to us, something we heard proclaimed in both testaments. For some of our group, it seemed like a risk to work with "gospel" as proclaimed in the Hebrew Bible, but we decided it was a risk worth taking. After all, Jesus would have grown up hearing these Scriptures. With the theme of risk in the air, the Book of Ruth surfaced in our conversation, as I will explain later. For now, listen to Boaz.

Boaz speaks:

These women!

What a challenge!

They walked into my life

and the world was changed.

Think of Naomi, my kinswoman.

Filled with bitterness,

and who could blame her?

Husband long dead and buried in foreign soil.

Then both her sons die

a long way from home.

But is this your home, Naomi,

without bone of your bone,

flesh of your flesh?

Still, here she is,
filled with determination.
She took a risk coming back
with her barren life and her foreign ways.
She came back to face us, her family,
and in every familiar face
she meets a reminder of her loss.

But she calls us…
calls me…
to face her.
To face her loss.
To face her future as part of us.
She won't let us forget.
She calls each of us to face
what we fear the most –
to lose all that matters
and still to live.
What faithfulness,
what courage it takes.
She has dared God
to see her through.
To give her the gleanings of a life
just like I gave her the gleanings of my field.
Would I have such courage
to go back
in order to go forward?

Musical interlude

These women!
What a challenge!
They walk into my life
and the world is changed.

Think of Ruth.
From Moab.
Not one of us,
yet one of ours.
You have to admire her devotion.
She could have stayed home
and found a new man.
God knows,
she can attract attention...
my attention, at least.
But here she is, with her mother-in-law.
No jokes, please.
Ruth took her mother-in-law
for better or worse,
for richer or poorer.
Now here she is,
gleaning her future out of the scraps of my fields.
As a wee girl,
did she ever imagine such a future for herself?
Did she pray to any god
or wish on any star
for *this*?

But she calls us...
she calls me
to open my life...
to open my future
to include them both.
She won't let Naomi go,
no matter that she's bitter and tired.
The future God gives her
must include them both.
She dares God to make a place for them in this strange land.
What courage,

what faithfulness it takes to go forward
when you cannot see beyond the next step.
God dares me to make a place for them in my home.
Will I have such courage
to go forward into the unknown
and not look back?

Musical interlude

These women!
What a challenge!
They walk into my life
and the world must change.

I cannot let Naomi waste away in emptiness.
She is my kinswoman.
I owe her my faithfulness
even if it costs me a struggle
with her bitter tears
and my own fear of emptiness.

I cannot let Ruth sell herself to buy a future.
She belongs to us now.
I offer her my generosity,
even if it costs me the respect of neighbours
who reject her foreign roots
but covet her attention.
I will risk my standing in the family
and provoke my cousin to forfeit his rights
to her property.
And to her.
He will not want her…
I hope!
I want her
to have a place,

to have a future with me.

These women!
What a challenge.
Each in her own way is vulnerable.
Each in her own way, determined.
Each in her own way, remarkable.
They call me
to show faithfulness
and courage;
to rearrange my community
and my life
to make a place for them
where God can carry their sorrow
and bless them with new life.

Do I have such trust in God's promise for our future
that I will take one small step of faith today?
I must.
I do.
God being my helper.

Musical interlude

Reading between the lines

In our first planning conversation, the theme of taking risks was in the air. We thought that a commitment service was a valuable opportunity to reflect on the risks in our lives. Perhaps participants could make a commitment to face a risk lively for them, relying on the presence of God. The discussion was rich. We talked about the future and its unknowns, the risks involved in moving out when we could not be sure what would happen. At this point, a suggestion came to work with the Book of Ruth, finding in the character of Ruth a symbol of courage and commitment. She walked into an unknown country, trusting herself to a God not yet familiar to her. That God, our God, was committed to her future. Discussion grew intense. Yes, the kind of risk Ruth took is significant, but what of those people whose real risk was back home – a challenge to face familiar people in well-known situations? How could we honour *that* kind of risk in the same service? Our first planning meeting ended with people assigned to look for prayers and songs on our theme. Others were to consider how we might develop a dialogue between Ruth and Naomi. We hadn't worked out everything yet. We trusted that somehow the planning would come together the next day.

I left our meeting thinking deeply about this discussion. We certainly recognized in Ruth someone risking the future. Her commitment to Naomi became a commitment to Naomi's God and Naomi's people. As I reflected on the group's concern to recognize other significant risks, I saw in Naomi a symbol of someone taking a risk to go back home. She returned with nothing to show for her years in a foreign land. She would have been utterly dependent on family members and neighbours who might not even remember her. What a risk, even with Ruth as a companion! And then Boaz tapped on the window of my imagination, asking for attention. Boaz, too, took risks in the story. At first, he simply offered the gleanings of his field to these women who had walked into his life. But then, it turned out he fancied Ruth, an outsider to his people. He wanted her for his wife, but a kinsman had a prior right to claim her. His risks were all around him in his community and in their response to his choices. Though Boaz had not even surfaced in our group's conversation, I suddenly heard his voice reflecting on the layers of risk faced by each character in the story. I sat down and wrote the monologue before the next meeting of the group.

When we met again, group members reported their suggestions. We had a list of songs; ideas for prayers. Someone had found a good dialogue between Ruth and Naomi, telling the first part of the story in two voices. Then I shared the draft of my monologue. I was hesitant because I did not want to overshadow other plans. The group liked it, however. It could follow the dialogue between the women, sharpening our theme of taking risks. Together we edited some of its lines to fit more closely with our earlier discussion. One of the men in the group volunteered to read it in the service. Then it came time to design a symbolic action.

Someone proposed the symbol of a footprint, cut from paper and lettered with a verse from our text. These were to be claimed by participants as a symbol of readiness to risk the next step in their lives. In order to honour the different kinds of risks we face, we decided that the woman who read Naomi's part would take a basket of footprints to the back of the church. Those whose risk lay in facing something "back home" could walk back to her to claim God's promise. The character of Boaz stayed in the centre of the church to stand with those whose risk was in the present moment, a current challenge that surrounded them. "Ruth" took her basket of footprints to the front of the church, waiting for those who faced an unknown future. The musical interlude that had linked the sections of the monologue continued during this part of the service as people took up our invitation and moved toward the character who symbolized risk as they knew it.

The service was quiet and powerful. Certainly not every worshipper took up the invitation to join the symbolic action we had designed. However, the custom at the Abbey is for worship leaders always to offer people a way to make their commitment without moving from their seats, recognizing that for some a planned action may prove too difficult. As is often the case, the group who designed and led the worship were profoundly moved by their own participation. The man who took the part of Boaz told me he'd never done that kind of public reading before. I was astonished. He'd read the words with such feeling, such sensitivity. He'd made them his words, though I'd written them. The people who prepared prayers did an extraordinary job, lifting up the kinds of risk we face and God's promise to us in the midst of risky territory.

Many people who attended the service asked for copies of this monologue. Their interest in reading it again led me to conclude that even if a fairly small proportion of the congregation moved during the service (moving is a risk for many people used to worshipping in a stationary place!), nevertheless the theme was a profound and appropriate one. The service remains in my memory as one of the best experiences of planning worship with a group. The group was diverse. We met together only three times. Some people had never planned or led a service before. Yet these folks discerned wisely that there are very different kinds of risk we face. They wanted to honour the differences that would surely lie within those who came to the service. They proclaimed in a beautiful way that God is committed to us in the midst of all the risks we take. This is Good News.

Letting go

The MacLeod Centre hosts a number of school groups each year. Students, mostly in their early and mid teens, come with their teachers as part of classes in religious studies. Such school groups undertake many different activities at the centre – some focused on the religious history of Iona, some enjoying the island as space for recreation and creativity. The Iona Community's concerns for justice and peace often contribute a session on human rights or fair trade. Worship at the Abbey is also part of the learning as students observe Christian ritual to see what happens. Some students attend worship for the first time as part of such classes. I try to keep such young people in mind, using words to help them attend to what is happening.

This service was prepared for Ascension Day, which fell on the last full day of a week when we hosted the Belahouston Academy. Groups from this school have come to Iona every year since the MacLeod Centre opened in 1988. Some students earn the right to participate three years in a row, so in my final year on the island, I knew several of the young people. I had already seen the challenge it could be for some of them to leave the island well, wondering if they would ever be able to come back. These things were in my mind when I turned to the stories of Jesus' ascension. I chose to use the reading from Luke 24.50-53. My readers included a young person, a teacher and a staff member.

Then Jesus led them out as far as Bethany,
and lifting up his hands, he blessed them.
While he was blessing them
he withdrew from them and was carried up into heaven.
They worshipped him,
and returned to Jerusalem with great joy.
They were continually in the temple blessing God.

Voice One: Well, that's him, gone again. Disappeared in the cloud, didn't he?

Voice Two: Now what will we do?

Voice Three: What will we do without him?

Voice One: How will we know what to do? What to say?

Voice Two: If only I'd had the chance to ask him one more question.

Voice Three: If only he'd told us that story one more time.

Voice One: If only I'd said I was sorry.

Voice Two: If only I'd said how much I loved him.

Voice Three: If only.

Voice Two: If only.

Voice One: Let us pray:

O God, we live in the land of "if only."
When we do something that goes wrong,
we say, "If only I hadn't done that."

Voice Two: When someone walks away angry or hurt,
we say, "If only I hadn't said that."

Voice Three: When someone disappears from our lives,
we say, "If only we'd had more time."

Voice One: God, we live in the land of "if only."

Voice Two: If only we could set things right.

Voice Three: If only we could make a new start.

Voice One: If only someone loved us, we could do better next time.

Voice Two: If only.

Leader:
Dear friends, there is good news for the land of "if only."
God does love us, in spite of the mistakes we make.
God does love us, even when we don't get everything done.
God will set things right so we can make a new start.

If only we can trust God's deep love that we have seen in Jesus.

Chant or song

Today is Ascension Day,
the day we remember Jesus being taken up into heaven
forty days after he rose at Easter.
I imagine that when Jesus disappeared this last time,
his friends were a bit nervous,
even though the Bible says they were joyful.
They had so much hope at Easter when he came back to them,
ate with them again,
talked with them again.
He was no longer dead.
He was with them.
Yes, he gave them joy.
But this time they knew he had gone to be with God.
This time they had to let him go.
This time they had to trust
that Jesus would give them what they needed to go on.
His love,
his stories,
his spirit would guide them.
They had to let him go
so that Jesus could be present to his friends throughout the whole
    world.
He was no longer a local carpenter from Galilee
who became a radical rabbi
and a preacher who upset some folks and amazed others.
He is God the Word who speaks to us
in whatever language we speak
to tell us how important we are to the world God loves.
They had to let him go
so that *we* could hear this for ourselves
through his love,

through his stories,
through his Spirit.

Chant or song repeats

Sometimes we have to let someone go
so they can move on and find a new place where they can grow;
some place where they can make a difference;
some place where God needs them.

Friends sometimes have to let each other go
because we start to move in different directions
and make different decisions.
The friendship is still a gift, no matter how long it lasts.

Students and teachers have to let each other go
at the end of a school trip or a school year.
Sometimes we're glad to let each other go…
and sometimes it's hard.
Because working together can be a gift.

I remember when my favourite teacher left my secondary school
before I graduated.
I thought I was supposed to leave first;
I thought she'd always be there when I came back to visit.
I thought that's how teachers were supposed to behave.
But you know, she went back to university to study more science
and then she went to work for the government in Canada
as a scientist concerned about the environment.
And the government sent her to the United Nations.
Now she's one of the people
trying to get countries to agree to protect the world against climate
    change.
I'm very proud of her.
It's hard to believe she taught in my home town.
We had to let her go.

And the world is better for it.
The world has her gifts now, not just my home town.

Belahouston kids,
just imagine that one of your fabulous teachers could also change the
    world.
But you'd have to let them go.
Everybody, look around.
Imagine that someone you care about here
could move on and change the world.
But we'd have to let them go on
without us.

Friends and neighbours,
students and teachers,
parents and children,
colleagues and co-workers,
some day we have to let each other go.
So let us cherish the time we have with each other;
let us be thankful for the gifts we receive from each other.
And let us appreciate each other this very minute
so that when we do have to let each other go on to whatever comes
    next,
we do not end up living in the land of "if only."
Instead, let us make good memories together
that teach us how to live for whatever comes next.

Chant or song repeats

Invitation to communion:

Before Jesus left his friends
he showed them a way to remember him.
He gathered them around a table like this
and shared bread and wine with them.
Around a table we can remember good times with friends;

we can share stories.
We can even remember the folks who can't be with us –
people we had to let go;
people who have let us go.
But surely they are here with us
in the stories we remember about them
and the love and respect we hold for them.
And you know,
Jesus' friends who gathered around a table with him
were quite a mixed bunch.
Some friends got up from the table and let him down;
they got him arrested.
Some were too scared to stand up for him;
some stood by and watched what happened to him
and wondered what to do.
Still he loved them all.
So this is a table where good news is on the menu.
God does love us, in spite of the mistakes we make.
God does love us, even when we don't get everything done.
God will set things right so we can make a new start.
So join us
if you'd like to taste the good news of God's love.
Join us to give thanks for friends and neighbours around the table –
and for the people who join us as Jesus does,
through the mystery of love.

Communion can be shared

Prayer after communion:

When we have been touched by God's love for us around this table,
we can sometimes find the courage to let things go
and hand things over to God.
In this prayer, I invite you to do that
by taking a deep breath at any point in the prayer

that reminds you of something you'd like to give over to God.
Then breathe out in the silence that follows.
Your breath is your prayer.

Let us pray:

God, you give us the breath of life.
Your spirit prays within us through our sighing.
Tonight we let go of anything that we're worried about… (*pause*)
We give to you anything we're afraid of… (*pause*)
We trust to you the people we love… (*pause*)
And the people we'd like to help… (*pause*)

God, you give us the breath of life.
As we take one more deep breath,
let it be the breath of courage
to take us on from here.
Let it be the breath of courage to make a difference
because we've been here with you.
Let it be the breath of courage
because you are always right beside us, wherever we go.
Amen.

Reading between the lines

For this Ascension Day service, I chose to read the account at the end of
Luke's Gospel because it is told more simply than the parallel story in
the Book of Acts. It focuses on the visual moment of Jesus' disappearing
and the response of the disciples. I definitely took liberties with the way
Luke tells it to help my listeners imagine what some of Jesus' disciples
might have said or felt as they watched him disappear. Knowing that
many children present would never have heard this story before – and
many would not have celebrated Easter – I thought that the imminence
of their own leave-taking might be a point of connection. I was also
aware of a few students who were about to leave Iona for the last time,
having reached the age limit for this particular school trip. They had

expressed a little sadness to me already. Often young people feel things like this quite keenly but cannot give voice to those feelings.

I hoped in some way to gather up the ambivalence of leaving and letting go in the phrases beginning "if only." "If only" can be a kind of lament for people of any age who must go on, living in spite of regrets – indeed, living in the midst of regret. I knew that some children from this school had faced losses and gone through difficult family situations. Young people can punish themselves with a litany of "if only." I wanted to create a moment when participants could surrender regrets to God and hear an invitation to live differently in the future. The Church grew out of Jesus' followers' ability to accept such an invitation and build a community that makes a difference in the world in spite of their own weaknesses and regrets. It's an invitation we need to offer in worship again and again.

Working with the teachers from Belahouston Academy has given me immense respect for their commitment to their students and the effort they make to create opportunities for each student to grow in appropriate ways. While I was thinking about this special group of teachers, I remembered my favourite teacher. She had a similar commitment to inspiring our creativity and helping us imagine new possibilities for our lives. Then she ventured out on a path that took her out of teaching and into an international arena where, I'm sure, she has been trying to inspire diplomats and politicians to imagine new possibilities for the world. I remember when I learned about her new career, I was astonished as well as impressed. By telling a bit of her story, I hoped to invite the students of Belahouston to wonder about the potential in their teachers. Students so often cannot imagine that teachers are anything other than taskmasters setting assignments and giving grades. Yet, truly, Jesus invited all kinds of people to achieve potential others couldn't see in them. His ascension became the moment when the disciples had to live in a new way. I wanted to lift up the possibility for both students and teachers to imagine that any one of their group could set out on a path with world-changing consequences.

Yet even to imagine this means letting people move beyond our current relationships and expectations.

During the reflection, we sang an African-American spiritual with words very appropriate for Ascension Day. *"Over my head, I hear music in the air"* is a song with rhythms that children and young people love. It brings together the visible and invisible worlds of God's concern in an energizing way. In this service, I used it to keep the young people connected during my reflection, knowing they would not listen attentively for more than a couple of minutes at a time. At the end of the service, we sang the whole song again and the Abbey was rocking! The next day I heard some of the boys humming it again on the way to the ferry. Infectious music is a good way to plant seeds that may sprout later, when the time is ripe.

As is our custom on Thursday evenings, we celebrated communion around a long table on this occasion. I rewrote the traditional story of the Last Supper with images that might connect with young people from Glasgow. I wanted them to know that Jesus' disciples were from a rough-and-tumble world, too, not unlike theirs. The prayer after communion draws on the image of the Spirit found in Romans 5, connecting breathing and praying. For those unaccustomed to religious ritual of any sort, sighing and breathing may be one of the most accessible forms of prayer. I use this way of praying with much younger children, too. Whatever our age, I hope we can recall that the Spirit breathes in us whenever a sharp gasp or a long sigh reminds us of our need for God. Leaving Iona brings its own occasion for a long sigh. When our sigh expresses a bit of gratitude and a bit of regret, it is good to remember that the Spirit is still with us as we turn away from a special time in this holy place.

8

Amazing Space

A guest hurried over to me one afternoon as I walked through the Abbey cloisters.

"Nancy, where did you get that sweatshirt with the picture of Iona Abbey? I've been looking for one in every shop on the island."

I paused to give her question some thought. I knew I didn't have a shirt with a picture of the Abbey on it. The guest could see my puzzled look.

"You had it on this morning," she said. "You know, the one with the poem on the back."

A light dawned. And I began to laugh. "That shirt came from Saskatchewan."

Now it was the guest's turn to look puzzled. Saskatchewan is not one of the place names that Canada shares with Scotland!

"It's not the Abbey on the front of that shirt," I chuckled. "It's a grain elevator."

That someone could confuse a prairie grain elevator from the plains of western Canada with Iona Abbey will make many of us laugh in disbelief. If you could see the image on my shirt, however, the mistake would be more understandable. In a washable reproduction of a lovely painting by Saskatchewan artist Henry Ripplinger, a road curves toward the tower of the grain elevator in a way reminiscent of the path approaching Iona Abbey. That tower is square with a peaked roof, rather like Iona Abbey's signature Benedictine design. But the most striking thing about this picture is the sky. The tower is set against the deep reds and oranges of sunset, made more glorious by fingers of indigo clouds reaching across the expansive horizon. A gorgeous prairie sunset. The kind of sunset that sweeps across Iona in the summertime to fill another expansive horizon and bathe the Abbey tower in its blessing.

That someone could mistake a colourful prairie landscape for the beauty of Iona is also a reminder that the Isle of Iona is not the only place where we can pause to savour the wonders of God's creation. Iona Abbey is not the only towered structure from which hungry souls are fed. As I reflect on this mistaken identity and think about what I've read between the lines at Iona Abbey, I am struck by a parallel with Jesus' life of prayer. Jesus sought out the wilderness, the emptiness of the desert, to enter the fullness of God's presence. With its barren hills and wide-open horizons, Iona offers that same paradoxical gift – the empty wild filled with anticipation of something, *someone* more than we can see. Perhaps this is what George MacLeod sensed when he spoke of Iona as a "thin" place where spiritual and material worlds touch. Yet, as much as I have come to love Iona and the Abbey, I also know God's breathtaking presence in the vast prairie wilderness I call home.

To be empty and full at the same time – a paradox of our encounters with God, wherever they happen. Only as we empty ourselves and pour out to God our deepest longing do we find God filling our souls with living water that seeps into the well from which we draw our daily lives. Paradox beats at the heart of Jesus' identity, that very earthy life in whom the holiness of God takes flesh. George MacLeod points us to this paradox in his prayer: *"Invisible we see you, Christ above us, Christ beneath us, Christ beside us."* Only as we divest ourselves of what we expect Christ to look like are we given a glimpse of his surprising smile in eyes that meet ours – at our daily bus stop or in the exchange of his peace.

Looking back through my reflections, I am struck by several key paradoxes that I think name qualities characteristic of liturgy at the Abbey, woven into the overall fabric of worship there, not just this collection. These themes might serve as souvenirs of this journey, in a sense. They are not insights unique to the Abbey, but they become noticeable there through the Iona Community's intention to welcome so many different people to participate in worship together. They are commitments of hospitable worship. I hope you have found traces of the following qualities as you have read between the lines of worship at the Abbey with me:

— Worship explores *significant* themes in *simple* ways. The most profound truths and challenging insights can be presented in clear words, straightforward sentences and stories that have an impact on our daily lives. This may seem obvious, put so bluntly. Yet sometimes addressing a significant issue gets us bogged down in weighty words and arguments not easily grasped on first hearing. On the other hand, a simple approach can lead us into the shallow end of the pool when we long to dive deep. By presenting matters of great importance – to God and the world – in simple words and symbols, worship draws more participants into the depths of God's Word and wisdom.

— Every service of worship is full of *meaning* and *mystery*. Whether the theme is personal or political, daily life is held up for scrutiny and its meaning remade in light of God's Word. I always hope that people who have worshipped in a service I lead will leave with something to ponder and something to pray over. But this hope has sometimes led me to say too much, to explain too many things at once, to fill a service with meaning of my making. On Iona, I have come to trust more thoroughly the mysterious movement of God's Spirit in silence, in simple gesture, in the inspiration deep within us that we carry away to sustain us until we gather again. When we say less in worship, we may hear more from God's own mysterious ways. Not every truth can be brought into words. For what we cannot express, we have the Spirit's pleading.

— The rhythms of worship embrace both the *playful* and the *poignant* aspects of life. Laughter is a gift of God, and a light spirit can celebrate goodness or challenge arrogance in ways that energize our lives as Christ's followers. But the Man of Sorrows also draws close to us so that we can face the wounds in lives that touch ours and not draw back in fear or distress. Because our hearts hold both tears and laughter, our worship must help us offer both to God – not necessarily in the same breath but at regular intervals on our journey.

— Worship leads us on a path that is both *honest* and *hopeful*. By honest I mean unflinching, presenting to God the world as we know it, the predicaments we face, those of our own making and those more complex than a single life can fathom. By hopeful I mean that we confront these predicaments together, trusting that God's grace and our prayers can and will make a difference. If our worship isn't honest, it doesn't really matter. If our worship isn't hopeful, then our faith has lost its hold on God. Yet we can only risk facing the truth about ourselves and each other if we trust that God desires our well-being and is working in Christ to make that well-being possible for us all.

Within each of these pairs, the tension of paradox insists that one quality should not be sacrificed for the sake of the other. Appreciating paradoxical truths is an honoured dimension of Christian faith. For example, the Psalms remind us God is more vast than a galaxy of stars can tell us, yet knows us with intimate love. Ancient teaching held up Jesus Christ as the divine-human paradox, God's eternal Word born in flesh and in time. And the text of every life story tells us that each human being falls short of God's intentions and yet can love neighbour and enemy with compassion that defies common sense. These paradoxes respect God's mystery and freedom to "accomplish far more than all we can ask or imagine," as the Letter to the Ephesians puts it. Paradox insists that we follow Jesus in humility and confidence, sure that we will occasionally stumble, sure that Jesus will pull us to our feet and put us on our way again.

These are not grand or dramatic findings discovered at Iona Abbey. But then Iona Abbey is not a grand cathedral like Lincoln or Westminster. Its history lacks the dramatic destruction and recovery faced in Coventry. Throughout my time on staff, the Abbey tower wore a "hair net," scaffolding with a protective green netting that supported the stonemasons in their ongoing task of maintaining its ancient walls. (Alas, not so photogenic for today's tourists, yet crucial if the Abbey is to welcome pilgrims of future generations.) Even wrapped for restoration, however, Iona Abbey offers an amazing space for its ministry of hospitality. It is not a pretentious place, but it stands with humble confidence to welcome the thousands who come season by season. Its rough-hewn stonework provides a solid foundation for the flexible grace and the adventures of the Spirit that draw us in and move through us when we worship there. God has opened such amazing spaces throughout creation – places where the mysterious meets the mundane. What I found between the lines at Iona Abbey can fill the page of worship in any space, any place where God's people are willing to pour out our lives in praise and in prayer, sure that we will be replenished by God the Source, the wellspring of our lives.

I once heard a scientist in a radio interview address a little girl's question. "What happens when space ends?" she asked. The scientist explained that current thinking pictured space, in its vast expanse, curving in on itself. For the eight-year-old, he imagined his thinking like this: "If you travelled as far as you could go from where you are right now, you'd end up back where you started." As a theologian, I like this image. In God, we live and move and have our being. We are embraced by God, no matter how far afield we go. If we travel to the furthest reaches of outer space – or to Iona's amazing, gracious space – God will bring us back where we belong. To come to God is to come back to our true selves. Time on Iona is a place on our journey within God. Iona Abbey is a stopover. Whatever we learn on our journey, at each and every stopover, we bring back to the place God needs us. There we will find the invisible Christ waiting for us.

It is appropriate to take my leave of Iona at this point, in the hope that what I learned there will surface not only in these reflections but in the ways I plan and lead worship in places I cannot yet imagine. As you let go of this collection, may the Spirit open your eyes to look out on the spaces and places that surround you and recognize there traces of God's presence and promise.

A Parting Thought

Here is a final vignette from a week near the end of summer, a point in the season when I felt brittle with fatigue. It was a week when the Abbey was filled with music, even more than usual. On Tuesday night, I joined the prayers for healing a little early. I knew I needed something beyond my own energy to go on. I sat in the congregation, waiting for the service to begin. The musicians took their places, took up their instruments.

The music was so beautiful, I wanted simply to be held – and held, and held – in the healing embrace of that moment.

In a way, I still am.

The poem that follows emerged later that night. It sums up the spirit in which I compiled these moments from Iona Abbey. So many of them moved with an unpredictable power beyond what I anticipated. Reading between the lines has been a chance to look back and consider how God honours our creativity and yet will not be held captive by our plans. I am reminded of the prayer offered in the Abbey every Saturday morning: "O God, we ask not for what we want, but for what you know we need." God's grace is always a gift and, so often, a surprise.

When a moment is precious to us, we often want to tighten our grasp, to hold on firmly so that time can't escape. As I learned time and again on Iona, such a response arises from my fear and frailty, not from my trust in God's abundance. My time there was a gift I will always treasure. When my three years had run their course, though, it was time to go. To make space for others. To look with refreshed eyes at the possibilities God sets before me in other places. To live differently now because of then.

Invisible we see you, Christ around us.

When we leave Iona Abbey, this prayer resonates within us, perhaps with more certainty than when we arrived.

Invisible Christ, we will *see you again.*

Transfiguration
– a moment in Iona Abbey –

Candles flicker.
Silence grows.
We wait
for God to move.
The oboe
sets its haunting melody free,
wandering,
seeking,
aching
in our souls.
Its beauty
caresses,
embraces,
holds me
in that holy,
healing moment.

Let us build them booths,
these musicians,
magicians,
muses of the Holy Spirit.
I insist!
Let us keep them
here
with us
and hold this moment,
this beauty,
to replay it
again,
again,
again.

Forever
and ever!

Then I know.
I smile
at my presumption.
The presumption of disciples
caught up in mountain top wonder,
shrouded in beauty.
Let us build them booths, Jesus,
so that they will never leave us.

Transfiguration.
We have what has been given –
wandering,
seeking,
aching
beauty
that holds us;
heals us;
embraces us with hope.
We cannot coax
such holy wonder
to remain.
We can only live,
changed by its gift,
changed by its moment.
We can live
trusting that a gift has been given.
The gift will come again.

Nancy Cocks
Isle of Iona, August 2003

Index of Biblical References

I indicate when a biblical text referred to in the collection occurs in The Revised Common Lectionary, using its manner of notation. Some texts I drew upon are found in the Lectionary, but I chose them thematically, not with reference to their place in the Christian Year. I have marked those texts with an asterisk*. A few texts do not occur in the Lectionary.

Text	Page	Lectionary Reference
Genesis 18.1-8*	97 (Entertaining angels)	Year A Proper 6 [11]
Genesis 28.10-17	205 (The gates of heaven)	Year A Proper 11 [16]
Leviticus 19.17-18; 33-34*	152 (Just friends)	Year A Proper 25 [30]
Deuteronomy 6.4-5	115 (Doing your best)	
2 Samuel 11.27b–12.7a	194 (When the penny drops)	Year B Proper 13 [18]
2 Kings 2.9-13	127 (A double share)	Year C Proper 8 [13]
The Book of Ruth*	245 (They walked into my life)	Year B Proper 27 [32]
Psalm 139	49 (When God is with us)	Year B Proper 4 [9]
		Year C Proper 18 [23]
Matthew 5.42-45a*	75 (The way I am)	Year A Epiphany 7 [7]
Matthew 25.31-46	145 (It's just that easy)	Year A Reign of Christ
Mark 6.30-38	229 (Give them something)	Year B Proper 11 [16]
Mark 12.41-44*	90 (Is it enough?)	Year B Proper 27 [32]
Mark 14.3-9	221 (A beautiful thing)	
Mark 15.25	180 (He is crucified)	Good Friday
Luke 2.8-20	161 (To you a child is born)	Christmas Day
Luke 6.27-28, 32,36*	49 (When God is with us)	Year C Epiphany 7 [7]

Text	Page	Lectionary Reference
Luke 9.51-60	127 (A double share)	Year C Proper 8 [13]
Luke 10.25-28*	115 (Doing your best)	Year C Proper 10 [15]
Luke 10.38-39*	75 (The way I am)	Year C Proper 11 [16]
Luke 10.38-42*	97 (Entertaining angels)	Year C Proper 11 [16]
Luke 11.11-13*	75 (The way I am)	Year C Proper 12 [17]
Luke 14.25-26*	75 (The way I am)	Year C Proper 18 [23]
Luke 15.8-10*	194 (When the penny drops)	Year C Proper 19 [24]
Luke 18.1-8	135 (The widow's might)	Year C Proper 24 [29]
Luke 19.36-40	215 (The stones cry out)	Year C Palm/Passion Sunday
Luke 24.50-53	253 (Letting go)	Ascension
John 1.1-4, 10-14*	106 (Bread and stories)	
John 2.1-11	66 (Going through the motions)	Year C Epiphany 2 [2]
John 3.1-10	39 (Born again?)	Year B Trinity
John 4.5-26*	240 (Living water)	Year A Lent 3
John 12.2-3*	75 (The way I am)	Year C Lent 5
John 12.20-33	171 (Unless a seed dies)	Year B Lent 5
John 15.12-14*	75 (The way I am)	Year B Easter 6
Acts 9.36-42	185 (To be remembered)	Year C Easter 4
2 Corinthians 5.16-18*	39 (Born again?)	Year C Lent 4

There are three seasonal items that are not based on particular texts, but on themes of the day:

A parable for Advent	85	Advent
It depends how you look at it	58	Christmas
A parting thought	268	Transfiguration

A Selected Bibliography

Many books could be listed under each heading. I have chosen a handful of items that I found helpful in my reading, research and planning for worship and workshops.

The History of Iona

Bradley, Ian. *Columba: Pilgrim and Penitent.* Glasgow: Wild Goose Publications, 1996.

Herbert, Maire. *Iona, Kells & Derry: The History of the Monastic Familia of Columba.* New York: The Oxford University Press, 1988.

MacArthur, E. Mairi. *Columba's Island: Iona from Past to Present.* Edinburgh: Edinburgh University Press, 1995.

————. *Iona: The Living Memory of a Crofting Community 1750–1914.* Edinburgh: Edinburgh University Press, 1990.

Markus, Gilbert. *Adomnan's Law of the Innocents.* Glasgow: Blackfriars Books, 1997.

Ó Maidín, Uinseann. *The Celtic Monk: Rules and Writings of Early Irish Monks.* Kalamazoo, MI: Cistercian Publications, 1996.

Sharpe, Richard (trans.). *Adomnan's Life of Columba.* New York: Penguin Books, 1995.

Celtic Christian Heritage

Bradley, Ian. *Colonies of Heaven: Celtic Christian Communities.* Kelowna, BC: Northstone Publishing, 2000.

De Waal, Esther. *The Celtic Way of Prayer: The Recovery of the Religious Imagination.* New York: Doubleday/Random House, 1997.

Low, Mary. *Celtic Christianity and Nature: Early Irish & Hebridean Traditions.* Edinburgh: Edinburgh University Press, 1996.

O'Loughlan, Thomas. *Celtic Theology: Humanity, World & God in Early Irish Writing.* New York: Continuum Press, 2000.

Works by George MacLeod

Only One Way Left. Glasgow: The Iona Community, 1956.

The Whole Earth Shall Cry Glory: Iona Prayers. Glasgow: Wild Goose Publications, 1985.

We Shall Rebuild: The Work of The Iona Community on the Mainland and the Island. Glasgow: Iona Community, 1944, 1962.

The Iona Community – Its History and Vision

Ferguson, Ron. *Chasing the Wild Goose: The Story of the Iona Community.* Glasgow: Wild Goose Publications, 1988.

———. *George MacLeod: Founder of The Iona Community.* London: Collins, 1990.

Morton, T. Ralph. *What is The Iona Community?* Glasgow: The Iona Community, 1969.

Shanks, Norman. *Iona, God's Energy: The Spirituality and Vision of the Iona Community.* London: Hodder & Stoughton, 1999.

Selected Works from The Iona Community

The Iona Abbey Worship Book. Glasgow: Wild Goose Publications, 2001.

Iona Abbey Music Book (companion to the *Worship Book*). Glasgow: Wild Goose Publications, 2003.

Bell, John L. *Come All You People: Shorter Songs for Worship.* Glasgow: WGRG, The Iona Community, 1994.

————. *One Is the Body: Songs of Unity & Diversity.* Glasgow: WGRG, Wild Goose Publications, 2002.

————. *There Is One Among Us: Shorter Songs for Worship.* Glasgow: WGRG, The Iona Community, 1999.

Bell, John L. & Maule, Graham. *Jesus and Peter: Off the Record Conversations.* Glasgow: Wild Goose Publications, 2002.

Burgess, Ruth. *A Book of Blessings...and How to Write Your Own.* Glasgow: Wild Goose Publications, 2001.

Galloway, Kathy. *A Story to Live By.* Cleveland, OH: The Pilgrim Press, 1999.

Galloway, K. & R. Burgess, (eds.). *Praying for the Dawn: A Resource Book for the Ministry of Healing.* Glasgow: Wild Goose Publications, 2000.

Paynter, Neil (ed.), *This is the Day: Readings & Meditations from The Iona Community.* Glasgow: Wild Goose Publications, 2002.

Pickard, Jan Sutch. *Out of Iona: Words from a Crossroads of the World,* Glasgow: Wild Goose Publications, 2003.

Wild Goose Worship Group. *The Wee Worship Book, 4th Incarnation.* Glasgow: Wild Goose Publications, 1999.

Music Permissions

Take O Take Me As I Am – John L Bell

Copyright © 1995, Wild Goose Resource Group, Iona Community, Scotland. Used by permission.

Behold, Behold, I make All things New – John L Bell

Copyright © 1995, Wild Goose Resource Group, Iona Community, Scotland. Used by permission.

Ka mana'o l'o – Joe Camacho Arr. John L Bell

Copyright © 1999, 2002, Wild Goose Resource Group, Iona Community, Scotland. Used by permission.

Through our Lives and by Our Prayers – John L Bell

Copyright © 1995, Wild Goose Resource Group, Iona Community, Scotland. Used by permission.

Jesus Christ, Jesus Christ – IONA

Copyright © 1998 Wild Goose Resource Group, Iona Community, Scotland. Used by permission.

Reamo Leboga

WORDS: Tswana, Daisy Nshakazongwe; English paraphrase, Andrew Donaldson
MUSIC: Daisy Nshakazongwe, as notated by I-to Loh.
Tswana © 1986 World Council of Churches and the Asian Institute for Liturgy and Music. English © 2001 Binary Editions. (http://binaryeditions.com).
Music © 1986 World Council of Churches and the Asian Institute for Liturgy and Music. All rights reserved. Reprinted with permission.

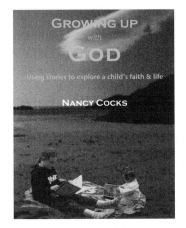

Growing Up With God
Using stories to explore a child's faith and life

How can you help children to 'grow up with God'? One way is through storytelling. By telling children stories that speak of their concerns, by listening to their own stories, and by exploring their questions, you can help them to grow up trusting that God will be at the centre of their lives.

Have fun getting to know Fergie the Frog and others through Nancy Cocks's wonderful stories as you and the children you care about find new ways to experience and grow closer to God in everyday life.

Growing Up With God is for parents and grandparents, teachers, ministers and priests – indeed for any adult who cares about the spiritual lives of children. But be warned: your heart will not escape untouched! What matters to children often matters deeply to adults as well. We all can learn to trust God's presence more deeply. Whatever our age, we can 'grow up' with God.

Nancy Cocks, a Canadian Presbyterian minister who has used storytelling in her ministry for over twenty years, was Deputy Warden with the Iona Community on the Isle of Iona at the time of writing this book. She is the author of the best-selling Fergie the Frog adventures for young readers (published by Novalis).

Meet Fergie the Frog!

Stories by Nancy L. Cocks
Illustrations by Jirina Marton

Fergie Tries to Fly

Frogs may not be able to fly, but they have other talents, as Fergie discovers when a baby bird falls into the pond.

Where Oh Where Is Fergie?

When two children frognap Fergie, will he ever find a way to return to the swamp?

You Can Count on Fergie

Fergie may not be the best at math, but when it comes to being a good friend, he gets top marks.

Nobody Loves Fergie

Fergie's big brother, Freddie, seems to be getting all the attention these days. Doesn't anybody love Fergie anymore?

Fergie Cleans Up

The swamp is a mess when human campers come to stay for a few days. How can they be so thoughtless?

Fergie Counts His Blessings

When Fergie misses Frog Scout camp because of math homework, he decides to run away and start a new life on his own.

Fergie Has a Birthday Party

Fergie needs one more guest for his party, but how can he invite a toad? Everyone knows frogs and toads don't mix!

Fergie Goes to Grandma's

Fergie would rather hunt gnats than go to Grandma's, but when he spends an afternoon listening to Grandma's adventures he realizes she's pretty special after all.

The Iona Community is ...

- An ecumenical movement of men and women from different walks of life and different traditions in the Christian church
- Committed to the gospel of Jesus Christ, and to following where that leads, even into the unknown
- Engaged together, and with people of goodwill across the world, in acting, reflecting and praying for justice, peace and the integrity of creation
- Convinced that the inclusive community we seek must be embodied in the community we practise

Together with our staff, we are responsible for:

- Our islands residential centres of Iona Abbey, the MacLeod Centre on Iona, and Camas Adventure Centre on the Ross of Mull

and in Glasgow:

- The administration of the Community
- Our work with young people
- Our publishing house, Wild Goose Publications
- Our association in the revitalising of worship with the Wild Goose Resource Group

The Iona Community was founded in Glasgow in 1938 by George MacLeod, minister, visionary and prophetic witness for peace, in the context of the poverty and despair of the Depression. Its original task of rebuilding the monastic ruins of Iona Abbey became a sign of hopeful rebuilding of community in Scotland and beyond. Today, we are about 250 Members, mostly in Britain, and 1500 Associate Members, with 1400 Friends worldwide. Together and apart, 'we follow the light we have, and pray for more light'.

For information on the Iona Community contact:
The Iona Community, Fourth Floor, Savoy House, 140 Sauchiehall Street,
Glasgow G2 3DH, UK. Phone: 0141 332 6343
e-mail: admin@iona.org.uk; web: www.iona.org.uk

For enquiries about visiting Iona, please contact:
Iona Abbey, Isle of Iona, Argyll PA76 6SN, UK. Phone: 01681 700404
e-mail: ionacomm@iona.org.uk

For more books and other items from Wild Goose Publications
Phone: 0141 332 6292
Website: www.ionabooks.com